581
M IL

Milne, Lorus

The nature of plants

DATE			
11-27			
MAR 8			
MAR 8			
5-18			
1/5			
5/28			
April 16			
10/31			
April 14			
3-22 86			
May 28			

THE NATURE OF PLANTS

Also by Lorus and Margery Milne

THE NATURE OF ANIMALS

WHEN THE TIDE GOES FAR OUT

THE PHOENIX FOREST

GIFT FROM THE SKY

THE CRAB THAT CRAWLED OUT OF THE PAST

GROWTH AND AGE

BECAUSE OF A TREE

FAMOUS NATURALISTS

THE NATURE OF PLANTS

Lorus and Margery Milne

Illustrated by Norman Adams

J. B. Lippincott Company
Philadelphia   New York

To Dottie and Pete, who enjoy the world
of outdoor plants, especially
Erythronium, Cypribedium, and *Hepatica.*

ISBN 0–397–31282–2

Copyright © 1971 by Lorus and Margery Milne

ALL RIGHTS RESERVED

Printed in the United States of America

Library of Congress Catalog Card Number: 78–151473

SECOND PRINTING

Typography by Jean Krulis

Contents

THE NATURE OF PLANTS

Giant redwood
and minute bacteria

1
The Sizes and Shapes of Plants

Plants include the smallest of living things and the largest, the shortest lived and the longest, the most productive of organic foods and the most destructive. If not for green plants and their processes of photosynthesis, the world would not be habitable for animals or mankind. If not for nongreen plants and their abilities as decomposers, life would soon run out of raw materials.

The smallest plants are certain bacteria that can live only as parasites on animals, in which they cause a disease called pleuropneumonia. When conditions are favorable, they reproduce by means of sporelike "elementary bodies" so small that if 254,000 of them were lined up in single file, the whole line would be only an inch in length. Each elementary body probably includes fewer than 1200 large molecules, counting those that constitute a cell membrane around its inner features. Its inherited control system suffices only to handle about forty different chemical reactions—those essential for survival, growth and reproduction. With virtually no spare parts, the elementary body is close to the lower limit of complexity necessary for life. Any minute dislocation of a molecule or two could disable the cell.

At the other extreme are the enormous big trees and coastal redwoods in California. One big tree measured 101½ feet around at 4½ feet above the ground. A redwood examined in 1963 was 368 feet tall and 44 feet around at chest height. Each of these trees contained hundreds of tons of wood, and probably was more than 3,000 years old.

The shortest life spans are those of microscopic bacteria where they have an abundance of food. In thirty minutes or less, a bacterium can grow to full size and divide into two— each a new bacterium ready to repeat the process. The longest lives, by contrast, are known among trees in the White Mountains of California and nearby in Nevada. Under the harsh climatic conditions on high slopes more than 9,000 feet above sea level, they grow gnarled and twisted. Yet growth rings in the wood of these old trees show that they sprouted over 4,000 years ago. The most ancient of them was not recognized until scientists cut it for study and learned, too late, that it was the oldest living thing. They had killed it at least 4,844 years from the time when it first took root.

Today we know that green plants need sunlight, carbon dioxide from the air, water, and very small amounts of mineral substances from the soil. The first experiments seemed to point to water alone. They were conducted by a Flemish gentleman, Jean-Baptiste van Helmont, who wrote in 1627:

I took an earthenware pot, placed in it 200 lb of earth dried in an oven, soaked this with water, and planted in it a willow shoot weighing 5 lb. After five years had passed, the tree grown therefrom weighed 169 lb and about 3 oz. But the earthenware pot was constantly wet only with rain or (when necessary) distilled water; and it was ample in size and imbedded in the ground; and, to prevent dust flying around from mixing with the earth, the rim of the pot was kept covered with an iron plate coated with tin and pierced with many holes. I did not compute the weight of the deciduous leaves of the four autumns. Finally, I again dried the earth of the pot and it was found to be the same 200 lb minus about 2 oz. Therefore, 164 lb of wood, bark, and root had arisen from water alone.

The idea that the nourishment of green plants came in part from the atmosphere was also proposed in 1727, when the English clergyman Stephen Hales suggested that gases could contribute to the increasing weight of the plant.

Of all living things, only green plants possess the ability to produce organic matter with light from the sun and with inorganic raw materials that occur naturally. Each organic compound contains carbon (symbol C) obtained from the carbon dioxide (CO_2) in the atmosphere, and hydrogen (symbol H) from water (H_2O), and energy, which holds the molecule together. For every molecule of carbon dioxide absorbed by green plants for use in photosynthesis, a molecule of oxygen (O_2) is released into the atmosphere. Animals that eat plants as food get energy by simplifying the organic compounds. They do so by processes in which oxygen is needed. For each molecule of oxygen the animal absorbs, a molecule of water and one of carbon dioxide are released. They contain hydrogen and carbon derived from the organic food.

Dead plants and animals, and their wastes (including fallen leaves), contain organic compounds that serve as nourishment to fungi and bacteria. These nongreen plants decompose the nonliving material, capturing energy from it. They too release carbon dioxide and water. Many of them need oxygen as well as organic foods.

Thus the green plants, through photosynthesis, provide the energy for themselves and all other living things by capturing it from sunlight. The green plants release oxygen, which is used for respiration by nongreen plants and animals. The carbon dioxide released by nongreen plants and animals cycles back to the green plants as raw material for photosynthesis. So does the water. All life is linked together in these ways.

THE PRODUCTIVE ALGAE—DELICATE AND TOUGH

Fully 70 percent of the oxygen in the atmosphere is there because of photosynthesis carried on by minute green plants drifting in the topmost 200 feet of the open oceans. Their importance to the world of life bears no relation to their size or relative simplicity. Features in the modes of growth and reproduction in these green plants show that they are most closely allied to the seaweeds and to some inconspicuous vegetation in fresh waters. For all of these plants the old Latin name alga, with its plural algae, has been adopted into English. Their most characteristic features are in their ability to carry on photosynthesis and to reproduce without roots, stems, leaves, flowers, fruits, multicellular sex organs or embryonic stages in development.

Algae differ greatly in the colored pigments they produce and in the chemical nature of the food reserves they store. Since these differences correspond to many features in reproduction and cellular details, scientists who study algae have assigned them to seven different primary divisions of the Plant Kingdom, each division called a phylum (see note page 13):

COMMON NAME	PHYLUM	PIGMENTS	FOOD RESERVE
Blue-green algae	Cyanophyta	green and blue	glycogen
Euglenoids*	Euglenophyta	green	gylcogen or paramylum
Green algae	Chlorophyta	green	starch
Golden-green algae*	Chrysophyta	green and golden	oils (lipids)
Golden-brown algae*	Pyrrhophyta	green and brown	glycogen or paramylum
Brown algae	Phaeophyta	green and brown	starch
Red algae	Rhodophyta	green and red	starch

* exclusively single-celled plants

NOTE: The classification of plants is well worth having in mind, so that information can be kept in scientific categories. The accepted grouping is based upon uniformities and differences in anatomical features. It reflects the past evolution of all members of the Plant Kingdom.

The kingdom can be regarded as consisting of two portions, each a subkingdom (see p. 29). A subkingdom is composed of major divisions called phyla (each one a phylum). A phylum is divided further into classes. Each class is composed of lesser categories called orders. Orders are subdivided into families. A plant family includes various genera (singular, genus). With genus and species the hierarchy of levels in classification comes to a convenient end.

The complete classification of an eastern white pine tree would be shown by

Kingdom	Plantae	(plants)
Subkingdom	Embryophyta	(embryophytes)
Phylum	Tracheophyta	(vascular plants)
Class	Gymnospermae	(gymnosperms)
Order	Coniferales	(conifers)
Family	Pinaceae	(pines and their kin)
Genus and species	*Pinus strobus*	(eastern white pine)

Western white pine (*Pinus monticola*) and red pine (*Pinus resinosa*) are other species of the same genus. Larch (*Larix laricina*) belongs to the same family as the pines. A redwood (*Sequoia sempervirens*) belongs to a different family of the same order. The maidenhair tree (*Ginkgo biloba*) belongs to a different order of the same class. Basswood trees (*Tilia americana*) belong to a different class of the same phylum. The seaweed known as sea lettuce (*Ulva lactuca*) belongs to the other subkingdom of the same Plant Kingdom.

Blue-green algae of about 1,500 kinds are widespread in shallow water, both salty and fresh. One called mermaid's hair grows on rocks and pilings that are exposed to air when the tide recedes. Under a good microscope, it is seen to be like all other blue-green algae in having its pigments dispersed uniformly through each cell and in having its hereditary material spread throughout the cell rather than isolated in a distinct nucleus, as in other green plants. Blue-greens reproduce only by ordinary cell division, with no indication of sexual activity. Many of them are held in threadlike lines or

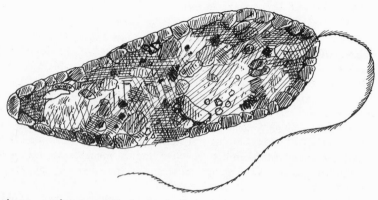

Euglena, a microscopic green cell

soft slippery balls by gelatinous materials in the outermost layer of the cell wall. A few blue-greens show an unusual ability: they capture pure nitrogen from their environment and incorporate it into chemical compounds. Some of these nitrogenous compounds escape into the surroundings and serve there as a fertilizer, aiding the growth of other plants.

Euglenoids are literally *Euglena*-like, and mostly denizens of fresh water—even stagnant fresh water. Of about 300 different kinds, the several members of the genus *Euglena* are the best known, perhaps because they become so abundant in stagnating ponds that they color the water green. Each of these single cells is extremely flexible and active. It lacks a cell wall, but has a nucleus, and special parts of the cell called chloroplasts because they contain the chlorophyll. Toward one end, the cell has a small pocket from which extend one or two long structures used in locomotion. Called flagella, they resemble whiplashes. To use them, the euglenoid extends its flagella and then curls them abruptly. This action pulls the cell along or rotates it in the water. The euglenoid reproduces without sexual activity. It produces a second pocket with flagella, divides its nucleus into two and splits lengthwise, sharing the nuclei and the several chloroplasts between the two new daughter cells.

Euglena and other euglenoids have been claimed by both

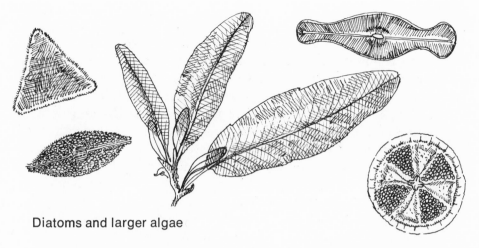

Diatoms and larger algae

botanists and zoologists. Rather than argue about whether euglenoids are more plant-like or animal-like, it may be better to recognize them as a style of life on the borderline between the Plant Kingdom and the Animal Kingdom. Some biologists regard euglenoids (and all other algae) as neither plants nor animals, but as members of a third kingdom—the Protista.

Green algae come in many shapes. Among the 6,500 different kinds, some are single cells, some threadlike filaments of cells joined in a single line, some spherical colonies one cell thick around a central cavity, and some in the form of thin sheets. Sea lettuce is one of them, found in shallow water along most of the seacoasts of the world.

The golden-green algae, which are called diatoms, outnumber all of the others in variety and as individuals. More than 10,000 kinds are known. They are the principal algae drifting near the surface of the sea, and coating submerged objects in brackish water and fresh. Each diatom produces around itself a delicate, two-part shell of transparent silica. The plant is not dragged down through the water by the weight of this inert covering, however. A droplet of oil buoys up the single cell, and also serves as a reserve of fatty food. When diatoms reproduce by simple division, each daughter cell inherits one half of the old shell. The daughter that gets the larger half soon secretes a new smaller half snugly inside; this combination provides for a new individual the same size as the parent cell. The other daughter gets the smaller shell half, and secretes a still smaller new part to fit inside; this individual is a size smaller than the parent. As the process is repeated over and over, progressively smaller individuals are produced. The final product seems to be a diatom too minute to manage on its own. It discards the shell half that it inherited and moves about until it finds another individual similarly unencumbered. The two unite in sexual fusion to form a single diatom of full size. This new cell secretes both halves of a new shell, and starts the sequence all over again.

Most of the approximately 1,000 kinds of golden-brown algae are whirling, flagellated cells called dinoflagellates. For much of the year they are second in abundance only to diatoms in the upper levels of the open sea. Occasionally they become extraordinarily abundant, coloring the water and poisoning it, causing people to complain of "red tides" that are killing all the fishes and sea turtles. Many dinoflagellates produce light, for no known reason. Some make the water sparkle in darkness around a swimmer or in breaking waves. Others glow more steadily and illuminate the sea where a school of small fishes is swimming at night.

Brown algae of about 1,500 kinds and red algae showing twice as much diversity are all multicellular, with complex programs of sexual reproduction. All but a few are firmly attached to the sea floor or to submerged rocks, the browns in shallower water than most reds. The browns include most of the conspicuous seaweeds, such as rockweed or bladder-wrack, and all of the tremendous kelps that grow along the cool coasts of the world. Generally the large brown algae are buoyed up by gas bladders that keep their bladelike expanses spread to the sun. Rootlike parts anchor the plant, preventing it from being washed ashore by storms. Red algae are usually more feathery. A few are exceptional in being coarse and more accessible from land. People harvest certain kinds as a source of a nutritious dry powder called sea-moss farina, used for making puddings or for thickening soups. A commercial extract called algin, which lends a rubbery, resilient nature to the cell walls of many red algae and brown algae, finds a market for giving a desirable consistency to hand lotions and low-fat ice creams.

THE SURPRISING FUNGI

The Latin word fungus (plural fungi) for a mushroom has given us the common name for a tremendous number of plants that lack chlorophyll and nourish themselves as decomposers or parasites. Like the algae, they grow and reproduce without roots, stems, leaves, flowers, fruits, multicellular sex organs or embryonic stages in development. Like algae, they come in many shapes and sizes. Together with the algae, the phyla of fungi constitute one subkingdom of the Plant Kingdom, called the thallus plants or Subkingdom Thallophyta.

Most minute of the fungi are the bacteria, classified as "fission fungus plants" (Phylum Schizomycophyta) because they are single cells that reproduce by crosswise division (fission). Like the blue-green algae, and perhaps related to them, bacteria have their hereditary material throughout the cell rather than isolated in a distinct nucleus, as in other nongreen plants. Three different shapes of bacterial cells were discovered in 1676 by the Dutch cloth merchant, Anton van Leeuwenhoek, who made and used some of the earliest microscopes. Commonest are the cylindrical rods, such as cells of the *Bacillus* that decomposes wet hay and

Fungi on a rotting log

those that cause tuberculosis. Abundant, too, are the spherical bacteria that are called coccus forms; they include the parasitic kinds that cause boils in man and mastitis in cattle, the disease agents of septic sore throat, gonorrhea and lobar pneumonia. Least common are the spiral forms, such as the rigid *Vibrio* of cholera and the long flexible spirochete of syphilis.

We tend to hear of the disease-causing bacteria because of the harm they cause. Actually, there are only about 150 kinds that give trouble to mankind or to domestic animals and plants. Ten times that many must be regarded as "harmless, useful or necessary" (in the words of the late Professor Otto Rahn of Cornell University) because they prevent the accumulation on earth of useless dead bodies and wastes. They return mineral matter to the soil, and recycle the carbon dioxide and water. A few kinds, living in enlargements called nodules on the roots of clover and other leguminous plants, capture important amounts of nitrogen from the air and release nitrogenous fertilizer into their vicinity.

Another 500 different kinds of fungi are called slime molds (Phylum Myxomycophyta). They seem to be close to the borderline between the Plant Kingdom and the Animal and were actually regarded as animals until their mode of reproduction was discovered. Those slime molds that live in wet woodlands germinate from microscopic reproductive cells called spores. For a few days the young slime molds creep about, engulfing organic matter and digesting it. Whenever they meet others of their kind, they join forces until the colony consists of a moving mass an inch or more long. Eventually the mass begins to dry out. At the same time it elaborates distinctive spore cases as much as half an inch tall. From these, the wind disperses the spores.

The great preponderance of fungi grow as slender, branching threads with few obvious features. Members of one group, called the alga-like fungi (Phylum Eumycophyta, Class Phycomycetes), can be recognized because the threads lack cross walls and appear to be branching tubes containing continuous cytoplasm and many nuclei. They distinguish themselves into about 1,500 different kinds when they reproduce by forming various kinds of spores. The common black mold of bread, which shows color only when its spores develop, is an alga-like fungus. So is the colorless or gray water mold that often attacks the gills of fishes in aquarium tanks. The downy mildew of grapes and the late blight of potatoes are both members of this group of fungi.

Sac fungi (Class Ascomycetes) and club fungi (Class Basidiomycetes) belong to the same phylum of plants, but rarely can be distinguished until they form reproductive parts following sexual fusion. Simplest in structure among sac fungi are the yeasts, which produced thin-walled spore sacs (asci) only at rare intervals. More obvious members of this class are the green molds on citrus fruits, which yield the antibiotic drug penicillin, and the edible morels and truffles, which grow from decay-causing threads on wood and other organic material in soil. Parasitic sac fungi cause scab on apples, chestnut blight, and the Dutch disease of American elm trees. Club fungi bear their spores in groups of four at the tips of special club-shaped reproductive cells, such as those on the "gills" of common mushrooms, or lining the tubular "pores" of bracket fungi, or in the central mass of puffballs. White pine blister rust, wheat rust, and corn smut are among the parasitic kinds of club fungi. More than 40,000 types of sac fungi and 25,000 of club fungi are known. In both classes, about 90 percent are decomposers that are harmless, useful or necessary to the welfare of other living things.

LICHENS—THE HARDY PIONEERS

Among the most famous partnerships in nature are those known as lichens, in which algae associate with fungus threads to mutual advantage. The algae may be blue-greens or greens, but the fungus is almost always a sac fungus—rarely a club fungus. Apparently either a broken piece from a lichen reaches a new location, perhaps blown there by the wind, or the new lichen begins where a fungus spore germi-

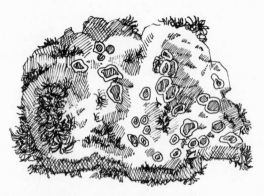

Lichens—a successful partnership

nates with some moisture and then, fortuitously, is joined by an alga being dispersed like dust by the wind. The fungus strands hold the combination in place, absorb water from rain, dew or fog to as much as 35 times the dry weight of the lichen, and release the moisture to the algal cells while photosynthesis is possible. The fungus also shields the algae from intense light and wind. The algae share the food they produce with the fungus, which otherwise could not continue growing without finding organic matter to decompose.

Some lichens appear thin as paint, and often as colorful. Others appear leaflike, affixed to a rock, a tombstone or the bark of a tree at only a few places. Still others seem shrubby, or hang in streamers from the branches of trees. Lichens hold their place easily in the wettest forests of the temperate and tropical zones. They grow more slowly on the rocky sides of high mountains where hard frost comes every night, and in the polar lands where winters last more than half the year. About 400 different lichens are known from Antaretica, compared to 2,200 from North America, and 18,000 for the whole world. The shrubby kinds known as reindeer moss form the principal winter food for caribou, reindeer, and lemmings. A leaflike lichen that breaks off and rolls before the desert winds in Asia Minor and North Africa is one of the plants credited with being the "manna" eaten by the Children of Israel. Other lichens, which are native to more northern lands, yield the dye known as litmus (which turns red in acid solutions and blue in alkaline ones) and the more permanent colors used in native fabrics, including the Harris tweeds of Scotland.

THE LOWLY MOSSES

When a moss spore alights in a suitable place and absorbs moisture, it sends out a green filament remarkably like some of the green algae that grow on wet soil. It branches a little, but then does two things that no alga can. From its lower surface it sends down colorless filaments called rhizoids that give anchorage. From its upper surface it develops budlike swellings that slowly grow upward, forming a stalk with leaflike plates of green cells on all sides. Eventually, the bud at the tip of the stalk opens to display multicellular sex organs. These may be a number of saclike bodies containing hundreds of sperm cells, or they may be flask-shaped, each containing a single egg cell. When rain or heavy dew provide water in which the sperms can swim to eggs, the eggs are fertilized and begin to develop as tiny embryos. Part of the embryo grows upward as a slender stalk bearing at its tip a complicated spore case. Soon the case releases spores into the wind.

The saclike organs which contain the sperms, the flask-shaped organs surrounding eggs, and the embryos all distinguish mosses as belonging to the other big subdivision of plants, the embryo plants (Subkingdom Embryophyta). Within it, they are members of the Phylum Bryophyta—the moss plants. In addition to about 16,000 different kinds of mosses, the bryophytes include about 8,500 kinds of liverworts and 300 of hornworts with similar features. These plants are mostly less than an inch tall, although clusters of them may spread over much of the floor of a forest. One reason for their lowly growth is that they have no stiffening materials. In a moss clump, the outermost branches lie nearly horizontal, against the ground, while those in the center of the clump are held upright only by leaning on adjacent branches on all sides.

THE FEATHERY FERNS AND THEIR ALLIES

Almost anywhere a moss can grow, a fern can grow taller. But unlike a moss, which has only rhizoids for anchorage, a fern produces roots, a stiff stem, and real leaves. The leaves characteristically uncurl from a bud. Until they have spread out they are called fiddleheads or croziers. Afterward, they are called fronds. Most fern fronds have a stiff midrib from which branching veins extend. Within the veins and midrib, special cells allow rapid conduction of water from the roots, and organic foods from the frond, to the rest of the plant. Often the edge of a fern leaf is deeply notched. If the notches reach the midrib, separating the thin green blade of the leaf into a series of parts (called pinnae) on each side, the frond is said to be pinnately compound. In many ferns the edges of the pinnae are similarly notched to the branch veins, making the frond twice-pinnately compound or even thrice-pinnately compound. The shape of the leaf is helpful in identifying the fern. About 9,000 different kinds of ferns have been found on earth, mostly in shaded forests and wet areas. A few float on water. In the Torrid Zone, which lies

Fern and moss plants

between the Tropics of Cancer and Capricorn, tree ferns as much as 60 feet tall are common.

The most distinctive feature of different ferns is the way they produce reproductive spores that the wind will disperse like dust. The spores develop inside special spore cases, which may be clustered along the edges of pinnae, underneath. Or they may be in little groups often called "fruit dots" below the pinnae, or in grapelike clusters on special parts of the frond or of fronds that bear only spore cases. The spores do not grow directly into new fern plants, however, even when they germinate on suitable surfaces with plenty of moisture. Instead, they produce small heart-shaped thin thalli with rhizoids below and multicellular sex organs. After sperms have fertilized the egg cells, new ferns develop by embryo stages that lead to formation of new fronds, stem and roots.

A similar life history, with characteristic differences, is followed by fern allies, such as whisk ferns (Subphylum Psilopsida), clubmosses (Subphylum Lycopsida), and horsetails (Subphylum Sphenopsida). Ferns constitute the Class Filicineae in Subphylum Pteropsida. The ferns and their allies, like the seed-producing plants with which everyone is most familiar, all possess special cells for rapid transport of water and organic foods. Collectively these cells are called vascular tissue. For this and other reasons such plants are classified in the Phylum Tracheophyta and known as vascular plants.

Ancestors of the whisk ferns were the most ancient of vascular plants. They grew exposed to air on mudflats about 400 million years ago. Others of their descendents became tall trees and grew in swamps during the Carboniferous period (the "Coal Ages"), which began about 345 million years before the present and lasted 65 million years. Fossils from these ancient times show that the tree-sized vascular plants of the Carboniferous were mostly enormous clubmosses, horsetails and true ferns. Decomposition could not keep up with the growth and death of these types of vegetation, and the residue became consolidated as coal. Today there are only 3 sur-

viving kinds to represent the pioneering Subphylum Psilopsida, about 800 clubmosses, and 25 horsetails; none of
them grow as trees, and most are less than a foot tall.

THE RESINOUS CONE-BEARING TREES AND SHRUBS

Fossils from late in the Carboniferous period include a
few trees with a new feature: they produced seeds. A seed is
an embryo plant together with a reserve supply of nourishment, generally enclosed in a waterproof coat. Having its root
ready to push out and its first leaves ready to unfold, a seed
can react quickly to conditions suitable for growth or remain
inactive ("dormant") for weeks, or years, or even centuries.

The world still has nearly 700 different kinds of trees and
woody shrubs representing the earliest class of seed plants.
Called gymnosperms (Class Gymnospermae) because their
seeds develop exposed—enclosed in no fruit of any kind—
they include the familiar cone-bearing vegetation such as
pines, spruces, hemlocks, firs, cedars, junipers, cypress and
redwood. All but a few are evergreen because they retain their
waxy leaves for more than a year—until after the leaves of
the succeeding year have expanded and are engaged in photosynthesis. Forests of these trees provide valuable wood,
which is man's largest crop. Lumbermen speak of the gymnosperms as "softwoods," despite the fact that trees they regard as "hardwoods" have the softest and lightest-weight
wood known, and that the wood of cypress and some other
"softwoods" is quite hard. Most gymnosperms have sticky resins in special canals within their bark and leaves. A great many
have sticky cones as well, in which their seeds develop. For
this reason they are called conifers—"cone-bearers."

THE HARDWOODS AND FLOWERING PLANTS

Most kinds of plant life today have flowers of some kind.
They produce fruits around their seeds, and for this reason
are placed in the Class Angiospermae. Features of the flowers
have allowed botanists to identify more than 285,000 types of
angiosperms. This is more than twice as many as all of the

Cones of needle-leaved trees

thallophytes, bryophytes, ferns and fern allies, and gymnosperms combined. The smallest angiosperms are the duck-
weeds and water meal that float on ponds. The vast majority
are much larger and grow on land. Consequently, when people who live on land think of plants, they usually think of
angiosperms. Much that has been learned about flowering
plants applies equally to the gymnosperms and to the ferns as
well. This justifies including all of these vascular plants in
the Subphylum Pteropsida—the "leafy plants."

Fossils preserved during the last 140 million years, beginning partway through the "Age of Reptiles," show that the
first flowering and fruiting plants were trees. Their flowers
resembled those of magnolias, with many large pale petals as
a display around a central, conical group of fruit-producing
parts called carpels. Between the carpels and the petals, the
flower spread a ring of stamens with golden pollen. Animals,
particularly insects, came to feed on sweet fragrant nectar
and expendable pollen, but rarely attacked the carpels. They
did, however, inadvertently transfer pollen from flower to
flower and brush it off against the carpels. This ensured
fertilization and production of seeds within the carpel wall.
By taking advantage of the abilities of animals to see, smell,
taste, learn and travel, the flowering plants greatly improved
the chance that they would bear seeds. By contrast, the gymnosperms continued to rely almost completely upon fickle
winds to disperse their pollen.

The flowering habit allowed angiosperms to change in
other ways and to colonize parts of the world that had previously been available only to the pioneering lichens. The tree
style of growth, which raised spores or pollen into the wind
for dispersal, was no longer essential. An insect could hunt
out the flowers on a low-growing herb, which made herbaceous growth worthwhile. Instead of spending many years to
produce a massive wooden trunk, a flowering plant could
mature in a season or two and use more of the energy it captured from the sun toward seeds and means for getting seeds
dispersed. It might grow, as so many annual plants do, from

the seedling stage to dispersing its own seeds in a few months of summer, and let the dormant seeds alone survive the winter. With no woody parts above ground, the flowering plant might grow for many years in semiarid lands and polar regions, benefitting from each season of warmth, moisture and sunlight.

Among the many kinds of flowering plants today can be seen an extraordinary diversity in form of flower and in groupings of flowers. One pattern of gradual change with time led to the buttercups, the geraniums, the mallows, the cacti, and the members of the carrot family which have their petals separate, and to the heaths, the primroses, the gentians, the morning glories and the daisies, which joined their petals into tubes with nectar at the bottom. These plants often have tap roots; their leaves ordinarily show a netting of

Flowers of dicot plants

Flowers of monocot plants

fine veins; their flower parts (sepals, petals, stamens and carpels) tend to be reduced in number to four (or eight) or five (or ten); their seeds have a pair of seed-leaves, called cotyledons, ready to unfold; these plants are called dicotyledons—or dicots, for short. A second great pattern led to the grasses and palms, the lilies and the amazing orchids. These plants generally have fibrous roots; their leaves normally have unbranched veins extending from base to tip; their flower parts tend to be reduced in number to three (or six); their seeds have a single seed-leaf; these plants are called monocotyledons—or monocots. About a fifth of the world's flowering plants are monocots.

GROUP OF PLANTS AND PHYLUM NAME	CLASS NAME	APPROXIMATE NO. OF KINDS
Thallophytes [Subkingdom Thallophyta]		
Blue-green Algae [Cyanophyta]		1,500
Euglenoids [Euglenophyta]		300
Green Algae [Chlorophyta]		6,500
Diatoms [Chrysophyta]		10,000
Dinoflagellates and kin [Pyrrophyta]		1,100
Brown algae [Phaeophyta]		1,500
Red algae [Rhodophyta]		4,000
Bacteria [Schizomycophyta]		1,600
Slime Molds [Myxomycophyta]		500
True Fungi [Eumycophyta]		[68,000]
Alga-Like Fungi	Phycomycetes	1,500
Sac Fungi	Ascomycetes	40,000
Club Fungi	Basidiomycetes	25,000
Fungi Imperfecti (sexual reproductive stages unknown)		1,400
Embryophytes [Subkingdom Embryophyta]		
Bryophytes [Bryophyta]		[24,800]
Mosses	Musci	16,000
Liverworts	Hepaticae	8,500
Hornworts	Anthocerotae	300
Vascular Plants [Tracheophyta]		[296,000]
Whisk Ferns [Subphylum Psilopsida]		3
Clubmosses [Subphylum Lycopsida]		800
Horsetails [Subphylum Sphenopsida]		25
Leafy Plants [Subphylum Pteropsida]		[295,000]
Ferns	Filicineae	9,000
Gymnosperms	Gymnospermae	630
Angiosperms = Flowering Plants	Angiospermae	[285,000]
Dicots [Subclass Dicotyledoneae]		235,000
Monocots [Subclass Monocotyledoneae]		50,000

2
Aquatic Plants

The largest plants of the watery world grow around the edges of the oceans, where the sea floor is no more than 60 feet below the surface. These are kelps with brown pigment concealing the green chlorophyll in their broad, leathery blades. Bending with each wave, they spread themselves as close to the air and sun as possible while remaining in the water. A heavy, ropelike part of the plant, as much as four inches in diameter, extends down to the bottom to a massive group of branches as big as a bushel basket. These branches are imbedded securely in the sea bottom and keep the kelp from being washed ashore.

To a diver in a wet suit, the kelps form an underwater forest. The brown blades fit together like a canopy of leaves, casting shade on the depths below. The shade would be darker if snails and sea urchins did not eat holes in the kelp blades, much as caterpillars would in a broad-leaved forest on land. More snails and sea urchins move up and down the ropelike parts of the kelps, which are the equivalent of tree

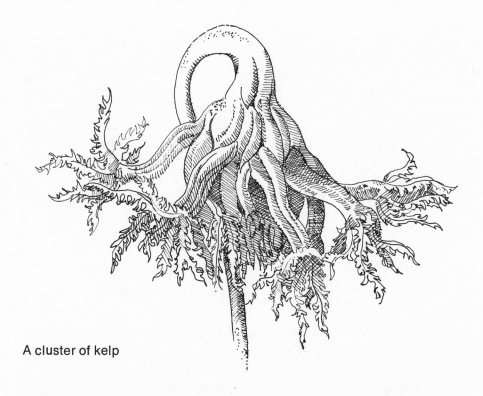

A cluster of kelp

trunks. Among them, fishes swim more casually than birds could in air. The water buoys them up, just as it does the kelp.

The water also absorbs light, and does so far more than air. Almost no red or violet components of the solar spectrum penetrate deeper than a foot or two. At ten feet below the surface, the orange has been absorbed and some of the yellow. Below twenty feet, the spectrum has narrowed to a band in the blue and green. At forty feet the green is missing, and only blue light reaches greater depths. The brown, ropelike parts of the kelps reflect no blue and appear black where they reach the sea floor. The floor itself seems dark blue, although samples of it brought to the sea surface are found to have many other colors as well.

In salty oceans and fresh water too, this diminution of the light at moderate depths largely determines what plants can live there. Almost no algae grow below the 200-foot level, because the blue light that remains is insufficient for photosynthesis. At great depths, and in the loose sedimentary material on the sea floor, the only live plants are decomposers. Virtually all of them are bacteria. For food they can rely upon dead bodies, and scraps missed by predatory animals, and solid wastes that descend silently like snow and accumulate on the bottom. Even at the greatest depths, bacteria perform this role. Although the pressure due to overlying water may be many tons to the square inch, the decomposers continue to simplify the organic matter. They get energy and raw materials for their own use, and release their own kinds of wastes, which become nutrients for other forms of life. Often these other forms are many miles away, and receive the nutrients because water currents carry the dissolved materials slowly from place to place.

DRIFTING AND SWIMMING PLANTS—THE "GRASS OF THE SEA"

In the topmost 60 feet of water, both in the open oceans and in lakes and ponds, minute green plants drift about freely where they receive solar energy each day. Commonest of them are the microscopic diatoms in their delicate glassy shells. Each shell half is pitted, as though for decoration, in a pattern so exquisite that only the finest microscopes can make it plainly visible. Yet the shells are useless to the many animals that eat diatoms. They discard the indigestible shells, which sink slowly to the bottom and there accumulate as a characteristic sediment called diatomaceous ooze. Nearly 12 million square miles of the ocean bottom are covered with this material, particularly between 45 degrees south latitude and the coast of Antarctica, and in the coldest parts of the North Pacific Ocean.

In some parts of the world, the fossilized remains of uncountable numbers of diatoms have been uplifted in thick deposits known as diatomaceous earth. One in northern Santa Barbara county, California, is more than 3,000 feet thick and extends over several square miles. This and smaller deposits in Nevada, Oregon, Denmark, France and North Africa, have been mined for years to obtain the commercially valuable

Ribbon kelp

siliceous material. It is used in abrasives, toothpastes, ultra-fine filters, and dynamite.

The droplet of oil with which a living diatom maintains its buoyancy and stays in the lighted upper levels of its water environment contains vitamin D, for which the plant has no known use. The minute aquatic animals that eat diatoms somehow retain the oil droplet and the vitamin, while digesting the rest of the contents from the diatom's shell. Larger animals that eat the minute ones again salvage the oil and vitamin. Fishes eventually do the same, and store the oil and vitamin in their livers. Cod-liver oil, and oil from the livers of halibut and sharks, remained the most reliable source for vitamin D as a supplement for human diets until the 1940's, when a synthetic substitute at a lower price was put on the market.

The living diatoms and other microscopic green plants drifting near the surface of the sea often become as numerous as 220,000 individuals to the quart of water. They have been referred to as the "grass of the sea," and have been compared to the number of grass blades that could grow on each small area of ground. Just as grass is the principal trap for solar energy on a grassland, so too in the illuminated levels of aquatic environments the microscopic green plants absorb the sunlight and incorporate some of its energy into organic compounds. They produce enough for their own needs and also a surplus that is the fundamental food for all of the animals in the sea and for the decomposers too.

The differences between a diatom and a grass blade are important in understanding the role of the drifting plants in surface waters. The diatom is a whole plant, a microbe that reproduces by dividing into two daughter cells with no old parent left over. So long as it can absorb light, carbon dioxide, water, and dissolved substances such as phosphates and nitrates from its surroundings, it can continue to grow and reproduce—unless it is eaten. When a diatom is eaten, the whole cell—the whole individual—is killed. But a grass blade is just a leaf on a monocot plant. If a cow or a grasshopper eats off the exposed part, the grass blade can grow more from its surviving portion next to the horizontal stem; the parallel veins in the blade make this particularly simple. Ordinarily the grass is not killed by supporting a herbivorous animal. Often the grass can complete its development and reproduce despite being a food resource to other living things.

The average diatom is less than 1/200th of an inch long, and most other drifting green plants in the surface waters are not much bigger. They are too small to be grazed upon by any animal the size of a grasshopper or a cow. Instead, the diatoms are food for minute animals that drift in the same waters. On the minute animals, in turn, crustaceans an eighth of an inch long or less feed actively. These animals are diminutive relatives of crabs and lobsters. Sardines, other herrings, and whalebone whales filter from the sea the small crustaceans wherever they are abundant. These fishes and whales, which are big enough to interest man, get just a small fraction of the energy that the green plants captured from the sun. A still smaller fraction is available to the larger fishes, the seals and toothed whales, and the squids that feed on the small fishes. But all of these animals contribute wastes and final remains upon which the bacteria nourish themselves by the processes of decomposition. In the end, all of the energy that the green plants captured from sunlight is released as heat and radiated to outer space. All of the nitrates, phosphates and other mineral materials absorbed from the sea by the diatoms and other drifting plants are freed again, to be redistributed by currents and repeat the cycle.

It is hard to think of plants benefitting from being eaten and killed. But without the minute animals to feed on the drifting plants, the green plants would cease to grow and reproduce after a week or two simply because they had used up all of the phosphates and nitrates in the sea water around them. The individual cells would just get older. Not until they died of old age and the decomposers could simplify their organic compounds would the phosphates, nitrates and other important materials be released again from being bound up in living plants.

Animals characteristically eat and kill more than they can absorb, and the excess goes to the decomposers along with more ordinary wastes and dead bodies. Where animals are numerous, the decomposers have plenty of food, and the simplification processes of decomposition release nutrients into the sea. This favors the growth and reproduction of the green plants that have not been touched.

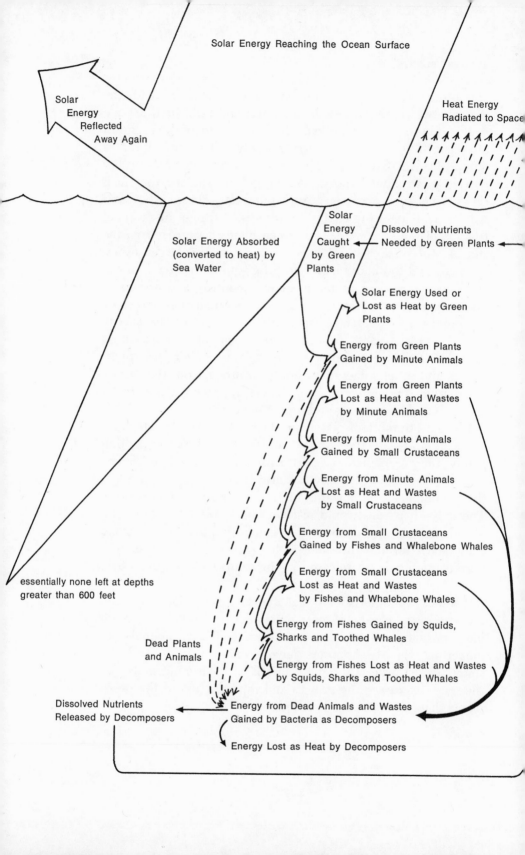

Solar Energy Reaching the Ocean Surface

Solar Energy Reflected Away Again

Heat Energy Radiated to Space

Solar Energy Absorbed (converted to heat) by Sea Water

Solar Energy Caught by Green Plants

Dissolved Nutrients Needed by Green Plants

Solar Energy Used or Lost as Heat by Green Plants

Energy from Green Plants Gained by Minute Animals

Energy from Green Plants Lost as Heat and Wastes by Minute Animals

Energy from Minute Animals Gained by Small Crustaceans

Energy from Minute Animals Lost as Heat and Wastes by Small Crustaceans

Energy from Small Crustaceans Gained by Fishes and Whalebone Whales

Energy from Small Crustaceans Lost as Heat and Wastes by Fishes and Whalebone Whales

essentially none left at depths greater than 600 feet

Energy from Fishes Gained by Squids, Sharks and Toothed Whales

Dead Plants and Animals

Energy from Fishes Lost as Heat and Wastes by Squids, Sharks and Toothed Whales

Dissolved Nutrients Released by Decomposers

Energy from Dead Animals and Wastes Gained by Bacteria as Decomposers

Energy Lost as Heat by Decomposers

THE RESISTANT SEAWEEDS

Where the resistant seaweeds grow, the storm waves crash against the shore. Each receding tide bares the rocks, rough ones and smooth ones. It lets the sandy beaches and mudflats drain and dry, perhaps bake in the sun. Many living things are stranded and die, only to have their dead bodies reclaimed by the sea and ground by wave action into particles small enough for decomposers to attack effectively. This adds a special wealth of nutrients for plants in the shallows. Additional phosphates and nitrates and other dissolved mineral matter arrive in the outflow from every river and saltmarsh.

Yet these benefits have matching dangers. Storm waves can rip at the sea floor where the seaweeds have their holdfasts, and toss these aquatic plants ashore beyond the reach of the highest tides. Seaweeds and fragments torn from them form a line of debris called storm wrack high on the beaches of the world. It gives some shelter and shade to beach animals. Until it dries too much, it serves as nourishment for the maggots of kelp flies.

Among the whole seaweeds and fragments left by recent storms or by the receding tide, the beachcomber can often find a good sampling of the plant life just offshore. Almost any place in the world, sea lettuce will be there. It is pale green, in thin sheets from 2 to 16 inches wide, loosely ruffled in a radiating pattern from the area by which it formerly was attached to some solid object on the sea floor.

Where the water offshore is warm, as it is most places between the tropics, many seaweeds grow at depths to which a person can wade easily and see the bottom in full natural color. Bright green tufts known as merman's shaving brushes are often 6 inches tall, the fine branches in the top yielding to the water movements. Smaller, fan-shaped, stiffer fronds resemble small shelf fungi. Generally their green is marked with concentric bands of brown that record changes in growth in different seasons of the year. Concealed in the muddy bottom may be long runners from which narrow branching blades 2 to 3 inches long emerge into the clear water, each one narrow and barely firm enough to stay erect. In protected places, often in quite shallow water when the tide is out, clumps of mermaid's wine glasses grow, each "glass" with a slender stalk 2 to 4 inches long, topped by a circular part resembling the corresponding portion of a champagne glass. A few feathery red algae inhabit the warm shallows too, each a bright pink and so softly feather-like that it holds its shape only while immersed.

Cooler waters north and south of the tropics favor the presence of coarser algae, both reds and browns. Particularly along North Atlantic coasts from the Maritime Provinces of Canada to Iceland, Ireland, Scotland and Scandinavia, a shrubby red (or brownish or purplish) alga known as Irish moss grows in dense clusters. At low tide right after storms that have kept fishermen from venturing out to tend their nets, great windrows of this alga often line the shore. People old and young hurry to gather the seaweed, to rinse it in fresh water and spread it out to dry on racks. The dry product has a market value for the organic chemicals it contains, and can be used locally in traditional foods. Related, but different, red algae called dulse and laver are more often saved as additions to the diet of coastal people.

Along some of these same shores of the North Atlantic, one of the coarse brown algae is similarly gathered for human food. Known variously as badderlocks, henware and murlin, it is often almost black after brief exposure to air among the storm drift. Its flattened frond with a central midrib may be 10 feet long and connected by a tough ropelike part with short side blades to a branching holdfast. Frequently the alga is thrown ashore because it attached itself when young and small to a sea mussel instead of a rock. After the badderlocks grew big and a storm tossed it violently to and fro, it tore the mussel away from its support and both were thrown together on the shore to die. If the alga and the mussel get too much pounding in the surf before being cast out of the sea, only the seaweed may remain because the violent water breaks the mussel's shell into small fragments. The rubbery nature of the seaweed saves it from similar damage.

Sea colander or shotgun kelp are the names given to a rather similar seaweed, the blade of which is perforated by holes of many sizes and the stalk of which bears no small blades on each side. Beachcombers often suspect that sea colander has been attacked by snails and sea urchins, but its holes are natural. They may reduce the dragging effect of large waves when the sea colander attains a length of more than 5 feet.

Ribbon kelps have no such holes unless animals have eaten through their tough rubbery blades. Usually they lack a midrib too, although a single blade may be 15 feet long and nearly 1 foot wide. On a large plant of this kind, the branching holdfast is often big enough to surround a baseball. Its fingerlike extensions ordinarily fit tightly into crevices of a rock in the sea floor beyond the line to which the water withdraws at the lowest tides of the year.

The intertidal zone of rocky shores in both the North Atlantic and North Pacific oceans is largely draped with the brown algae known as bladderwrack or rockweeds. One whose branches are smooth, dark greenish brown, and swollen at intervals with gas bladders inside, is sometimes distinguished as knotted wrack. Another, with pairs of gas bladders at the tips of branches and on opposite sides of the midrib too may be familiar to coastal people by its scientific name *Fucus*. The bladders of *Fucus* have a pebbly surface. At the center of each tiny bump is a minute pore from a small chamber within the wall of the bladder. In season, sperm cells swim out or in through these pores to attend to sexual reproduction of the seaweed. In spring, farmers along the coast sometimes gather quantities of rockweeds to work into the soil and let it decompose as fertilizer.

Along Asian coasts of the North Pacific, people actually "farm" the cool waters for the coarse brown alga, selling the dried plants to chemical companies. Along the Pacific shores of

North America, the chemical companies send out special boats to harvest the coarse kelps that grow naturally. The commonest are among the largest and best known of these brown algae. One with the scientific name *Macrocystis* is generally called just "giant kelp." Its holdfast may be 60 feet below the surface, and its thick ropelike stalk 150 feet long. Along both sides of the stalk where it turns to lie horizontally, short branches with globular floats the size of oranges support flat brown blades 10 feet long or more. Another, often known as "sea otter's cabbage," has a similar stalk from its holdfast but only a single float, 8 to 10 inches in diameter, from the surface of which many long narrow blades stream out almost horizontally in the water.

Far more unusual, and of little economic value, are the flexible sea palms that grow upright, attached to rocks in the surf zone. Each stalk is 1 to 2 feet tall, and supports a crown of narrow brown ribbons that hang down like the leaves on a real palm tree. Sea palms yield to every wave that crashes over them, but rise again as the foamy water withdraws. Constantly wet, they live where few animals can stay long enough to eat them.

Some of the red algae and a few greens that grow attached to rocks near the low-tide level feel gritty when rubbed between thumb and forefinger. They absorb large amounts of calcium from the sea, and deposit lime within their tissues or as an outer crust. In the tropical Pacific world and the Indian Ocean, they contribute a major share to the production of reefs. The reefs, in fact, should be called coralline reefs (for the coralline algae) rather than coral reefs, because coral animals provide a smaller share in the gradual accumulation of limestone. Under a hand lens, the stiff fronds of coralline red algae show a jointed character suggesting the parts of an animal's breastbone or backbone; at the joints the plant can bend when struck by a wave or when it is pushed against by a fish. Fragments of these plants do break off in large numbers, however, and are common among the bleached remains of life in the storm wrack on the upper beach.

FLOWERING PLANTS IN SALTY WATERS

For a very long time, the algae were the only seaweeds. No other type of plant made a mark in the fossil record until about 400 million years ago. Then especially adapted forms of vegetation began spreading onto land, into air and wind, away from waves and tides and salty water. But eventually— less than 60 million years ago—some of the descendents of the land plants began a reinvasion of the sea. Like alumni coming back for a class reunion, they tried out their abilities to fit into an environment that once had seemed the whole world.

None of the ferns or horsetails or clubmosses showed this new tolerance for salt around their roots. Neither did any of the gymnosperms. But of the flowering plants, a number of dicots and many monocots spread over the mudflats, into the tidal gutters, where every storm at sea sent waves that threatened their survival. Some became adapted to total immersion. Others retained the habit of trees, and formed dense swamps along protected coasts. All of these flowering plants added to the surfaces upon which diatoms and fine filamentous algae could grow, still further increasing the productivity of the tidal waters.

The flowering trees that grow into the sea are mostly mangroves. But the word "mangrove" identifies a way of life and a habit of growth, rather than a scientific classification, for members of four different families of plants have invaded the salt waters in this manner. Those of tropical coasts of the Atlantic Ocean are the red mangroves and the black ones. The branches of red mangrove tend to arch out over the water and send down strong roots called mangrove knees. Almost centipede-like on these supports, the plant marches in slow motion into deeper water while sediments collect around its roots and extend the land. Among the surprises to be seen from a small boat close to the edge of a mangrove swamp are the tree oysters that cling firmly to the knees where the tide covers them twice a day. Over and between these bivalves, sea snails and crabs creep about, browsing on the algae that coat every surface.

Coastal mangrove

Black mangroves thrive in somewhat shallower water, and produce separate upright trunks. The roots extend horizontally in the muck on the bottom, and send up many slender breathing organs not much thicker than a lead pencil. These show that, although the mangrove can tolerate the salty water around its roots, it needs more air than is available in the muck.

In the temperate zones of both hemispheres, a hiker who takes a shortcut across a mudflat at low tide is likely to hear the bright green plants underfoot crunching and breaking as though they were glass. The plants are glassworts, with leafless upright stems that are plump, jointed, and frequently branching in a pattern that has earned another name: chickenclaws. Inconspicuous flowers and fruits appear late in the season. When autumn frosts begin, the green color of glasswort is concealed by a brilliant red which gives the marsh the appearance of being on fire. Then the plant is likely to be

recognized by still another name: samphire. It is a member of
the family to which beets and spinach belong. A surprising
number of its close relatives live on salt deserts of all continents. One, called sea-blite, is a common weed on sandy,
salty beaches all over the world. Like glasswort, sea-blite
absorbs most of the water it needs from the humid air and
soon dies if transplanted to better soil with fresher moisture
if the air is dry.

The glasswort on the mudflat is often found between a
dense stand of cord grass or marsh grass on one side—toward
drier land—and a tidal gutter partly carpeted by eelgrass on
the other. Farmers along the Atlantic coast of the United
States used to cut the cord grass, which they often called salt
grass, as food for their livestock. They piled the cut grass
between upright poles driven into the mud, to prevent high
tides from washing away the fruit of their labors. When the
winter arrived and the marsh surface froze hard enough to
support a horse-drawn wagon or sled, they could come back
for the hay. By then it might be thoroughly dry.

Left to itself, the cord grass of the salt marsh might seem to
contribute no more to the living world than a shelter for musk-
rats and nesting waterfowl. It certainly favors the reproduction of salt marsh mosquitoes and other biting flies. But
at the same time and through seasons when no birds are
nesting nor are insects active, the productive grass supports
incredible numbers of decomposers. Products of partial decomposition are washed by rains into the tidal gutters and
there nourish, directly or indirectly, the young of important
fishes, crabs and shrimp that fishermen later are happy to catch
well offshore. Without the grass and the nursery shallows,
these types of seafood cannot maintain their numbers. They
depend upon the energy the salt marsh offers, like a subsidy,
to the welfare of coastal life.

The eelgrass or grasswrack maintains its fibrous roots in the
muddy bottom, while its narrow green leaves point whichever
way the current is going. Each leaf is about a quarter of an
inch in width and from 1 to 5 feet long. In season and where

the salinity is not too high, the eelgrass releases threadlike
pollen grains and captures them to set seed, all underwater
and in tune with water movements. This plant is the favorite
food of various kinds of geese, for it grows in similar situations
all over the world. Along the Atlantic coast of North America,
it formerly supported great flocks of brant, which are smaller
than Canada geese and lack the distinctive white cheek marks.
But during the early 1930's, when drought on land produced
the "Dust Bowl" in the semiarid Southwest, the eelgrass died
off from a disastrous disease caused by a slime mold. Most of
the brant starved or failed to reproduce, and this once-common
bird almost disappeared. Now both the eelgrass and the brant
have recovered to some extent, and scientists realize from their
research why these aquatic plants died off when they did.
Eelgrass resists the disease and produces its strange underwater flowers only where the flow of a river keeps the concentration of dissolved salts less than that in the open sea.
When drought reduces the river flow, the plant is exposed to
saltier water than it can stand. The result can be disastrous to
many kinds of life.

In tropical lagoons and river mouths, plants that resemble
eelgrass grow similarly. Like eelgrass, they are not grasses at
all. The manatee grasses, which are sought out by large water
mammals known as manatees or sea cows, belong to the same
family of pondweeds as eelgrass. Turtle grass, upon which
sea turtles feed extensively and among which tropical fishes
hide, is a member of the frog's-bit family, most of which grow
in fresh waters. But until they produce their inconspicuous
flowers, only a skilled botanist can know one kind from
another. The flowers reveal differences that have remained
almost unchanged for millions of years, while the plants that
produce them colonized in aquatic situations with a taste of
the sea.

Along many a tropical coast, the local people say that a
coconut palm will grow well only where it can hear the sound
of the waves. Certainly many of these palms lean out over the
beach where their huge fruits will have a chance of being

carried away by storm waves. No one really knows where coconut palms originated, for they have colonized the most remote tiny islands all around the world. Left awhile on a beach in the sun and humid air, the big seed inside its buoyant husk will extend a strong root and then a few green leaves. The first leaves are simple, broad, with prominent lengthwise veins. Later the young tree produces at ground level a huge bud. Its diameter will be that of the tree from then on. From it the pinnate leaves of the coconut tree expand, identifying it as a "feather palm" rather than a "fan palm." Soon the tree will begin the schedule it is to follow for the rest of its life— a period of some forty years. It will drop an old leaf and open a new one, using the same cells in the trunk to carry water to the new that it used for the old. The palm has no way to produce new conducting tubes, which explains why its trunk remains almost the same size all the way from the ground to the crown of leaves.

Feather palm
and fan palm fronds

ATTACHED PLANTS OF FRESH WATERS

At the edge of a river or a lake, as in the spray zone close to a waterfall, the world of aquatic plants merges almost imperceptibly with that of terrestrial life. Mosses spread from the margins of streams into the torrent. Certainly they are water mosses when they cling tightly to rocks and stay low, where the speed of the stream is slowed by friction. They get the light they need, carbon dioxide and more water than they can use. Yet mostly they grow slowly. By containing distasteful substances they repel aquatic animals that might eat them.

Mayflies in their immature stages and other insects creep about, staying low in the same way to escape the force of the rushing water. They browse on the thin film of algae and diatoms, which coat the same rocks. The green of the plants is almost imperceptible.

Close to the stream, plants of very many kinds thrive in the wet soil. Ordinarily we think of them as land plants, although they grow best where their roots are usually surrounded by water. In the temperate zones this is the habitat of bluebells and of forget-me-nots. According to legend, forget-me-nots got their name from the last imploring words of a gentleman who fell into the river while trying to pick some of these flowers for his lady.

Where the river broadens and slows to a gentle pace, willows and alders commonly overhang its banks. These trees tolerate spring floods that fling debris against them and threaten to wash away the soil between their roots. They resist the erosion to a remarkable degree, and retard the pace at which a valley ages through normal geological processes.

Cattails and bulrushes in temperate countries, like sawgrass and other sedges along river banks between the tropics, are less able to stand against a vigorous current in any season. Yet in some parts of the world, such as the Everglades in southern Florida, they occupy dozens or hundreds of square miles. The huge marsh of sawgrass in the Everglades has shallow water that drains very slowly southward because it stands on an almost horizontal table of limestone.

Anglers who like to keep their feet dry close to where fishes swim are usually familiar with plants that grow in the water at its very edge. Arrowhead, which gets its name logically from the shape of its leaves, and pickerelweed with its upright pointed clusters of purple flowers, keep their perennial stems and buds and roots deep enough to be unthreatened when winter ice covers the pond or stream. By midsummer their leaves and flowers extend into air, and provide perching places for dragonflies.

Wild rice is a grass that grows in shallow parts of lakes with a muddy bottom. Fishermen generally avoid it. But American Indians knew when to come to harvest the delicious grain. In their canoes they approached carefully, bent the heavy heads of the rice over the side and struck at the plants, shelling out

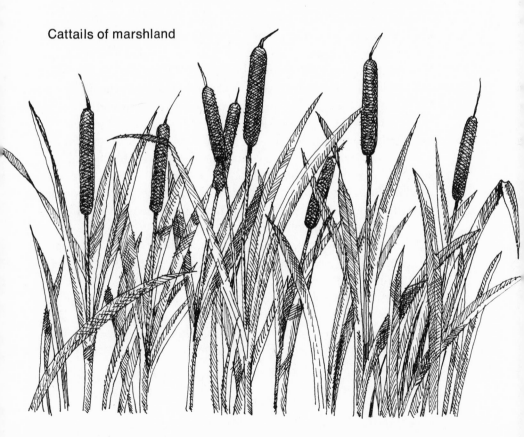

Cattails of marshland

the rice into the canoes. Later they scooped it up and stored it for winter food.

Water lotus grows in water more than 4 feet deep, too, but elevates both its foliage and its flowers above the stream or lake. Its conical fruits eventually bend over and break off. They float away inverted on the water surface while the holes in which the seeds have ripened enlarge and let the seeds drop out. Occasionally one reaches a suitable place in which to germinate, and escapes being eaten. Some lotus seeds that got caught in a Manchurian bog remained inactive for many years. For a while after scientists discovered these seeds and got them to germinate, the duration of their dormancy was supposed to have exceeded two thousand years. But later, better measurements of the radioactive carbon-14 in other seeds of the same batch indicated that 150 years was a more realistic length of the time during which they lay dormant. It is still an impressive record.

Water lily leaves gain the benefits from two worlds, with the top surface exposed to air while the underside is wet. Even the extra weight of a frog sitting on a lily pad while waiting for insects to come along may be buoyed up by the leaf, which has air chambers inside. Long leaf stalks connect the floating leaves to a thick, loglike stem embedded shallowly in the bottom mud. In autumn the stalks shorten, pulling the leaves below the level to which ice will form. After the ice melts again, the stalks elongate, returning the leaves to the water surface. In season, the water lily extends flower buds on similar stalks from the buried stem. Extending them through the water surface, the plant opens them where insects are likely to attend the pollination.

Many of the aquatic plants raise only their flowers into the air, while their leaves (and their fruits too) stay submerged. One called waterweed or ditch-moss has slender branching stems from which bright green veinless leaves arise in opposite pairs or in a continuous spiral whorl. In late summer the plant shows small white flowers with three petals where flying insects can reach them. But what good this does the plant remains a mystery, because pollen-producing flowers are on separate plants and these are exceedingly rare. A closely related plant known as tapegrass produces grasslike leaves as much as 6 feet long, and two kinds of flowers. The pollen-producing flowers break off and float around at the water surface. There they reach the fertile flowers, which are tethered by long slender stalks. After pollination takes place, the stalks curl like coiled springs, drawing the fruit underwater to ripen.

Water milfoil suggests soft green furry tails under the water, for the leaves that arise from the branching stems are deeply divided. Milfoil means uncountable leaves. People who raise tropical fish in aquaria often have a few stems of water-milfoil, or of waterweed, to give their pets places to hide and a generous supply of oxygen from photosynthesis. Occasionally, even in a fish tank, the water-milfoil produces its inconspicuous flowers close to the stem between its leaves and later a nutlike fruit with a single tiny seed in each of its four chambers.

Far coarser and harsher leaves with similar subdivisions grow from the submerged stems of bladderworts. These strange plants are named for the bladders or traps with which they capture mosquito wrigglers, small crustaceans and other

The half-wet leaf of a water lily

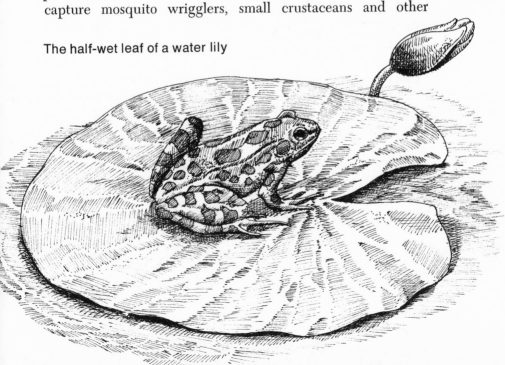

active water animals of less than a quarter inch in length. Each dark bladder is borne on a leaf or a side branch, and extends a few stiff bristles close to its trap door. If some creature bumps into the bristles, the door swings inward so quickly that the victim and some of the water surrounding it are sucked into the trap. Immediately the door closes again, and the plant starts secreting digestive juices around the animal. Soon the victim dies and digestion liquefies parts of its body, ready for absorption as nourishment for the bladder-wort. While all this is going on below the water surface, the plant may be extending stalks with flowers into the air. Flying insects are attracted by the pink or yellow petals, and inadvertently attend to pollination for the plant while seeking nectar.

THE BOG-MAKERS

Most of the other carnivorous plants in temperate and arctic regions are associated with a moss that can float on water. This is peat moss, or sphagnum, which comes in many different colors: green, golden-yellow, rusty brown and shades in between. When wet, as it usually is, its branching stalks are too soft to support themselves alone. But each leaflike branch consists of two kinds of cells. Some are the living parts of the plant, with chloroplastids carrying on photosynthesis in the light. Between them are special cells with strengthening in their walls, and an open pore to the outside world. So long as these cells are filled with air, they buoy up the peat moss. A dense mat of the moss can support a full-grown person, a great many bushes, and some trees such as larch or black spruce that can tolerate bog water around their spreading roots.

Below the living peat moss is dead peat moss, and cells full of water. Yet the dead cells exude organic materials that make the water acid, coffee-colored and unsuited to most kinds of life. In a closed lake or pond, where no current carries away these poisonous materials, decomposers soon cease to act and organic matter accumulates upon the bottom. Pollen, blown by wind from the trees around, may fall on the water and sink where it is preserved almost indefinitely. Botanists who specialize in studying pollen can learn from the layers of it at the bottom of ancient lakes what kinds of trees and other plants grew nearby during the centuries while peat moss gradually replaced the water with vegetable debris.

To walk on the boggy roof of moss over a lake is to tramp on "trembling earth." At every step the adjacent trees sway madly. Under the weight of a foot, the moss may sink enough for dark water to appear. Yet these are the places in which to hunt for pitcher plants and sundews that catch insects and digest them. The pitcher plants hold water in their vaselike leaves, and are well adapted with slippery internal surfaces and downcurved hairs at the top to prevent any insect that blunders in from escaping. Sundews work on a different principle. Reddish points from their leaf edges are tipped by clear glistening droplets of adhesive. If a fly or an ant gets caught, the leaf points curl toward one another and surround the victim. They hold it until digestion and absorption are complete, then let the drained dry body blow away. Taking from captured animals the nitrogen-containing nutrients they need for growth and reproduction, the carnivorous plants never risk taking in anything from the poisonous water surrounding their roots.

THE FREE-FLOATERS

Although coconut palms and mangrove trees and some lesser plants as well make use of water currents to disperse their seeds, only a small and select assortment of vegetation makes free-floating a way of life. Least appreciated of them today is a native of South America called water hyacinth. It was introduced accidentally into southern Florida, and now often chokes the drainage channels of the Everglades. The same kind of plant, and some others from the Old World, have almost roofed over the waters behind Kariba Dam on the Zambesi River in southern Africa. The roots of water hyacinth dangle into the water, while swellings filled with gas in the leaf stalks act as floats, keeping the leaves themselves spread in air. In South American waters, wherever manatees are numerous, they eat the water hyacinth and keep the drainage system open. If these big herbivorous animals are killed off, the plant becomes a weed.

The smaller floating plants are simpler in structure and so specialized that their true nature is harder to recognize. A floating fern with almost circular leaves in twos or threes has a tuft of true roots hanging into the water below the foliage. A floating liverwort has a shinier upper surface, and only clear rhizoids consisting of slender filamentous cells below. The larger of the two flowering plants that are still smaller is duckweed, which has a short root or two extending a fraction of an inch below its quarter-inch leaves. The smallest is water meal, with leaves not more than an eighth inch across and no root at all. Both duckweed and water meal store starch in the late summer until they are heavier than water and sink to the bottom. Living on this store all winter, they get thin and light again by spring, ready to rise to the surface as soon as the sun warms the water and shows that summer is sure to come.

3
Land Plants

Most kinds of plants live, as we do, on land. By spending the whole year out of water, they encounter climate. The sunlight is more intense, and causes the temperature to rise and fall much more rapidly and extensively than in any aquatic environment. Wind comes in gusts, sometimes bringing clouds of dust, or freezing rain, or sleet, or heavy snow. Even when the rain comes gently and is warm, the supply of moisture varies greatly, by the hour, the day, the week, or the month. Often before the plants can use the water for their needs, dry air takes it away. Each combination of available moisture and of temperature during the growing season, of exposure to wind, and of length of summer, constitutes a different environment for plants. Responding to these opportunities, the plants on continents and islands have diversified far more than those in all of the seas and fresh waters.

The underlying pattern of moisture distribution follows geological features. These affect the routes of storms and prevailing winds, just as they do of ocean currents. Air that moves down a mountain slope or from cooler lands toward the Equator picks up moisture, and deposits little. Air moving in the opposite directions, upslope or toward higher latitudes, often brings precipitation. The form of the land has much to do with drainage and the rate at which soil moisture disappears from around the roots of plants.

Throughout the world, whenever the amount of moisture reaching the soil during the whole of the growing season is at least four times as much as the air can evaporate and carry away, forests are the natural vegetation on continents and islands. In a temperate land, 30 inches of rainfall annually may suffice to support a forest. In the tropics, the precipitation must be greater because warm air absorbs more water than cool air does. On some tropical rain forests, nearly an inch of rain comes almost every day, for a total of 300 to 400 inches annually.

Trees of few kinds can grow where the climate provides water only during half of the growing season. In these places, they form no forests but grow separately with large areas of grass in between. Unlike most trees, the grasses can go dormant when the moisture gives out. All of their exposed parts die, while those underground or the seeds survive. In the temperate zones, an annual rainfall of 15 inches will usually support a flourishing grassland if the rains come in spring and summer. If the precipitation arrives mostly as winter rain and snow, not even the grasses can match the annual program. Then the land becomes clad in thornscrub or chaparral, which consists of harsh woody shrubs with special adaptations that resist the long summer drought.

Parts of the world with less than 10 inches of average precipitation challenge plants even more. Rarely does this little moisture come at a rate of an inch or less each month. Commonly none arrives at all for a year or more. Then a downpour, like a cloudburst, drops far more water than the plants or the soil can absorb. The temporary excess rushes away, eroding the land, and drought returns. Under these conditions, only a desert plant with special adaptations can grow.

It must resist desiccation or escape the prolonged dry periods in some way.

On most deserts, there is more moisture than shows in a rain gauge or on an instrument that measures the relative humidity by day. The extra comes as dew at night, when the temperature falls rapidly. But few desert plants possess suitable foliage with which to capture and absorb the dew. Instead, most of them have waxy surfaces exposed to air, reducing their loss of moisture when the air around them is heated by the sun. Below ground, their roots spread out and often occupy all of the spaces that are available. Any water that sinks into the ground after a rain encounters a root and is promptly absorbed. A big saguaro cactus in the American Southwest can store as much as a ton of water. To accommodate so much the leafless stem swells until its accordion-pleating almost disappears. The clusters of sharp spines along the lengthwise ridges still give the plant protection from the larger animals that might attack to eat the moist pulp inside.

In grasslands and forests, the plants affect the climate to a surprising extent between their foliage and the ground. The grass blades prevent wind from reaching the soil, but allow free vertical movements of air that bring them carbon dioxide. Some of this gas, which is so essential for photosynthesis, comes from decomposition of plant materials in upper levels of the soil. By being narrow and often vertical, the leaves capture energy from the oblique rays of the sun early and late in the day. But they let the light slant between them and heat the soil when the sun is high. At night, they let the radiant heat escape again and the ground cool quickly. The air among the grass blades may reach its dew point, and dew distill on the plants. They absorb this moisture readily, and compensate to some extent for the amount of water they lost by evaporation to the dry air during the day before.

In California, many hillsides within 30 miles of the coast are now grass-covered where less than a century ago great redwood forests stood. Until the trees were cut, the mists that wind blew ashore from over the cool current in the Pacific

Ocean met shiny evergreen needles and condensed to liquid. The moisture dripped to the forest floor and kept the air between the tall trees continually humid, favoring the growth of ferns and other low plants with delicate foliage. The soil, which was thick with fallen and decomposing needles, stayed moist. After yielding quantities of water to plant roots, it still had a surplus to run off in clear streams and small rivers. A rain gauge placed under the trees actually collected 30 to 40 inches more water annually than one beyond the forest, which received only the infrequent rains and no drops from foliage overhead. Now that the trees are gone, the mists continue inland and evaporate. Plants that need much moisture cannot grow. The soil has become thin and dry, with no continuous streams.

THE FOREST-MAKERS

Forest trees follow an ancient way of life, one that dates from more than 340 million years ago when the first tall plants formed swamp forests during Carboniferous times. Each tree grows as though guaranteed that every year would bring a good growing season, with suitable temperature and rainfall. During its first year, the tree grows much like any other seedling. But it does not mature and begin reproducing that year, or the next, or the next. For a dozen years or more the young tree grows upward toward the sunlight. All of the energy that it can accumulate goes into producing a sturdy wooden trunk with outstretched branches.

At first, almost every cell in a tree is alive. But as it grows, the dead cells of the outer bark become more numerous. The innermost wood, which is called the heartwood, dies without showing much other change. In a big tree, the heartwood and the bark account for most of the bulk. The only living cells are then in the inner bark, in the outer sheath of wood (the sapwood), and in the young twigs and leaves at the ends of the branches. Unlike an animal, all parts of which are of essentially the same age, a tree has old parts left from the years when it was young, and also new parts less than a year old.

The new roots, the new conducting tubes in the inner bark and the sapwood, and the new twigs and leaves of a tree that is 150 years old are just as young as those on a tree of the same kind at age 15 years.

A tree may be 15 years old before it produces its first few reproductive organs, such as cones or flowers. It will continue reproducing thereafter for the rest of its life, whether this is normally 40 years or 4,000. Some years its crop of seeds may be more numerous than in others. Often, one tree of a particular kind (perhaps a chokecherry or a larch) produces more seeds in odd-numbered years than in even-numbered ones, as though drawing excessively on its reserves of energy in one year and recovering in the next. This variation makes it difficult to estimate, for example, how many acorns a red oak tree produces in its lifetime.

A great many seeds are eaten by animals or destroyed by bacteria and fungus diseases. Yet even the seeds that germinate in a forest have a poor chance to survive. Thousands of the seedlings starve for lack of light on the forest floor. A rabbit or a deer might come along and eat all of the exposed parts of the seedling, killing it. At any one place in the forest, a hundred years may go by before a tall tree dies of disease or topples for some other reason, letting the sun shine to the ground. The seedlings in that small area benefit in the next growing season, and begin competing for the lighted space. For awhile, several may continue their upward race. Eventually one wins out. It fills the gap in the forest canopy left by the dead tree, and shades the others below it. They weaken from malnutrition, and become susceptible to diseases that are fatal.

In the continental United States and Canada, four different types of forests occupy separate areas. In the extreme west are the redwoods, which grow only where they receive cool foggy air. In the Southeast are pines, such as the longleaf and the shortleaf and the loblolly, which provide valuable timber. They are maintained by frequent fires along the ground, which do little harm to the pines but kill young trees of other

Coniferous
trees

Leaves,
deciduous
and evergreen

kinds. If left to grow, these others (such as liveoak, hickories, black walnut, and the hornbeams) would gradually replace the pines with a rich forest of broadleaved trees, including a great many that are evergreen.

The largest evergreen forest on the continent is of coniferous trees. It spreads like a sash diagonally from northernmost New England to Alaska and down to lower latitudes by growing at higher altitudes in the mountains there. It is best known for its spruces and firs which, while young, are favorite Christmas trees. At larger sizes they are harvested for pulpwood to supply the paper industry. In the Pacific Northwest they include gigantic Douglas firs and Sitka spruces that attain a height of more than 300 feet. Except for the coastal redwoods, which grow to be more than 380 feet tall, and one kind of Australian eucalypt at 365 feet, these are the tallest trees in the world.

These northern and mountain evergreen trees are particularly well fitted to tolerate heavy snow. Their branches extend horizontally or slope downward toward the tips. Lower, older branches are longer than new ones, which gives the tree a conical shape. When snow adds weight to the needles, the branches sag until each rests on the one below it and the lowest branches press against the ground. Wind can scarcely penetrate the snowy covering. The temperature of the evergreen needles may be scarcely below the freezing point each day in winter. Often they can carry on some photosynthesis with light that shines through the snow.

Downslope on the mountains and farther south in the eastern states, the forests consist of broad-leaved trees such as maples, oaks, beech and poplar. Red cedars, along with sumac and birches, grow where the forest has been leveled recently by a fire. Hemlock tolerates the shade under the broad-leaved trees where no fire has come for many years. But the hemlocks and red cedars are generally scattered and become conspicuous as evergreens only after the broad-leaved trees have dropped their leaves in autumn. By remaining bare all winter, the latter greatly reduce the surface area through which they would otherwise lose water by evaporation. This adaptation is important to let a broad-leaved tree survive where drought in late summer is followed by winter so cold that movement of water from the roots to the branches is slow—too slow to match an evaporative loss through broad leaves as well as the needs of photosynthesis. Each deciduous tree remains dormant until the longer, warmer days of spring let it move water more easily. Then it puts forth new foliage and makes up for lost time.

THE SPRING WILD FLOWERS OF THE DECIDUOUS FOREST FLOOR

Even before the winter's snow has all melted or evaporated in the warm sun that shines through between the branches of the leafless trees, lowly plants of many kinds begin extending fresh foliage and colorful flowers. No other forests produce such a delightful carpet of spring wild flowers. Until the leaves expand on the high branches of the deciduous trees and shut off the light, these special plants of the forest floor have their chance to engage in photosynthesis and to attract insects as pollinators. The lily family is particularly well represented, with dogtooth violet, trilliums, false lily-of-the-valley, Solomon's seal, bellwort and wild oats. The arum family contributes skunk cabbage, which is the first to open its flowers, and the jack-in-the-pulpit. The buttercup family has many members on the forest floor: hepaticas, goldthread, wind flowers, and wild columbines that attract ruby-throated hummingbirds to their heavy, nodding blossoms. The orchid group includes several kinds of lady's slippers and the charming showy orchid, which is widespread—particularly under hemlock trees.

Most of these wild flowers live precariously. In their short growing season they must gather from the sun the energy they need for expansion of flowers and the ripening of fruits and seeds. They must also accumulate a reserve on which to survive during the rest of the summer and through the winter, with enough energy left over to use in producing the next year's leaves and flower buds. If an animal eats all of the

Spring
wildflowers

exposed parts on one of these plants, or a person picks the whole stem with its leaves and flowers, the plant usually dies. Even if it can call upon a little remaining food in its underground parts and produce another leaf or two, it starves for light because, by then, the deciduous trees will have closed the canopy overhead for the season. Just above the wild flowers, an additional layer of fern fronds will have spread out from peculiar buds that unroll as they expand.

Hidden below the ferns, which need only a modest amount of light, are other spring wild flowers that get their energy at a still different time of year. They are the wintergreens and partridgeberries with waxy foliage that stays green through the winter. Under the snow these leaves get enough light to carry on photosynthesis while the temperature around them, beneath the white blanket, is barely above the freezing point. The light warms the evergreen leaves next to the ground, causing the snow in contact with them to melt. The plant is then in a close-fitting greenhouse in which the air is saturated with water vapor and well supplied with carbon dioxide from decomposition in the upper levels of the soil.

PERCHING PLANTS AND CLINGING VINES

In almost any forest, a few kinds of plants specialize in perching on the trees or clinging to them, getting closer to the light without expending energy in producing a sturdy trunk. Lichens grow on the outermost bark or drape downward from the branches. Each lichen is a double plant—a mesh of fungus threads enclosing masses of algal cells. The fungus holds the combination in place, and acts like a sponge for rain or dew. The algal cells use the water, along with carbon dioxide, in photosynthesis, and manufacture foods that nourish both partners. The lichen has no need to absorb anything from its support and, for this reason, can grow on a dead tree as well as a live one, or a rock face or a telephone wire that receives a similar amount of moisture and light.

Mosses generally grow better on the upper surface of horizontal limbs, where rainwater does not drain away so quickly after a shower and dust accumulates, supplying mineral nutrients. Some of the climbing ferns find a place for themselves in similar situations. Among these plants is one of the polypody ferns often called the "resurrection plant" because in dry weather its small leaves curl up and appear dead, only to revive and spread out again in the humid air after a good rain.

In tropical forests where rain comes almost every day, the number and variety of perching plants and clinging vines exceeds most expectations. In addition to lichens, mosses and ferns, each large horizontal limb on every tree supports orchids and members of the pineapple family (bromeliads). These flowering plants grow with only the wetted dust and the decaying remains of dead vegetation for a soil. The bromeliads, in particular, retain quantities of rainwater at the center of their whorl of stiff leaves and, for this reason, are called "tank plants." To the water come tree frogs and toads, dragonflies and mosquitoes to lay eggs in the "tank," and many animals of the treetops (such as monkeys) to get a drink without going to the ground far below. Sometimes small shrimplike crustaceans climb the tall trees while the humidity is almost 100 percent, and swim around in the water held by the bromeliads as though it were a pool in a stream.

Some of the tropical vines germinate from seeds among the perching vegetation, and then send long woody roots downward 100 feet or more to the ground. These cable-like roots are lianas, and serve to reach dissolved mineral matter needed by the vines in the upper levels of the forest.

Getting mineral nutrients from the soil is difficult for plants in the tropical rain forest because of the heavy rains. These dissolve out and carry away the soluble materials almost as fast as the decomposers release them. Nor does the soil contain any appreciable amount of humus, which might capture the dissolved materials and hold them until plant roots could absorb them. The rate at which fallen leaves and branches decompose in the consistent warmth and plentiful moisture is so rapid that humus cannot accumulate. In consequence, the floor of the tropical rain forest is generally bare, slippery, red mud. Few seedlings can get a start on it. Those few are often bromeliads that hold their own water and catch their own dust as nourishment. They present stiff spreading narrow leaves with edges sharp as saws to the wild pigs and other hungry vegetarians upon the forest floor.

Walking through a rain forest, one sees the upright trunks of tall trees, and twisting lianas of many kinds, but few leaves less than 50 feet above the ground. Petals that have fallen from a tree or from one of the clambering vines in the sunlight high above may litter the soil for a few days. Yet there is no way to tell what tree or vine produced them. The live flowers, the flower-visiting insects and birds and bats, the ripening fruits and the fruit-eating bats and birds and monkeys and insects, are all in the treetops—invisible from the ground. Only along the bank of a river, or the side of a clearing that has been made in the forest, does the canopy of foliage curve downward within reach. Then it shows the tangled form and extreme density made famous by early explorers, who traveled by canoe, as a "jungle" that had to be hacked open to let a man go through.

PRAIRIE GRASSES AND DESERT PLANTS

The high plateau country of equatorial Africa still has large areas where the elephant grass grows higher than an elephant's eye, to a height of 9 to 12 feet. Elephants and antelopes of many kinds push their way through the tall grass, finding edible leaves and heads of nutritious grain. In North America until about a century ago, grasses of similar height grew along the eastern edge of the Mississippi River basin. Pioneering men on horseback rode through, unable to see over the grass or find the native animals that lived among it.

To the west on somewhat more arid land, visibility seemed endless over the lower grasses of the Great Plains. After midsummer, the wind rippled the grass to the horizon in all directions. Among it then were sunflower heads and ripening pods on lupines. Great herds of bison, of pronghorns and elk roamed over these Great Plains, which supported also count-less prairie dogs, prairie chickens and smaller birds. Perhaps 30,000 Plains Indians followed the grazing mammals, com-peting for meat with packs of wolves, solitary grizzly bears, and predatory animals of smaller size. Colonists moved in with seeds of favored cereal grasses, such as wheat and oats, with plows and guns and fences, then discovered by trial and error which parts of this vast territory were suitable for raising the cultivated crops. Ranchers took almost all of the remaining grasslands, and replaced the wild animals with domesticated kinds. By 1900, the bison and elk were gone from the Great Plains, and the wolves and grizzlies were disappearing fast. The pronghorns and the Indians had been fenced out. The settlers turned their attention to exterminating the prairie dogs and the smaller predators. Now it is hard to find a stand of the native grasses or a place where the surviving prairie chickens can come to court and raise their young in the tra-ditional ways.

With the exception of maize, which was adopted from the Indians as "Indian corn," the favored cereal grasses are all kinds that were domesticated 8,000 or more years ago in Asia Minor. Selectively they have been improved to meet special requirements, such as high yield of grain, resistance to fungus diseases, and an inherited program of growth that would match the seasons where man chooses to raise these crops.

Unlike the native grasses of the prairies, most of which were perennials and formed a dense sod of interlacing roots that resisted erosion by strong wind even after long periods of drought, the introduced grasses are annuals. Particularly after they have been harvested (or have died of drought that came too early), they give little protection to the soil. Where farmers have chosen to plow and plant the land with crops of this kind, only to be faced by dry hot weather and high winds, their farmland has simply blown away, exposing the unpro-ductive subsoil. The most disastrous examples of this kind affected Oklahoma and adjacent states during the 1930's, and became famous as the "Dust Bowl." The dry soil that blew away commonly built up as small dunes of dust downwind, smothering crops and extending the devastation. In just a few weeks, great areas changed from being misused grassland to become desert. Decades of special care have been necessary to reclaim the area, and to induce it to yield more suitable crops.

Excessive grazing by livestock can also create deserts where grasslands grew. Each grass plant has a limited surplus of energy captured from the sun. If its leaves are clipped off or trampled on too often in a season, it cannot maintain itself or reproduce. But even before it dies, it loses its ability to compete with vegetation that the livestock find distasteful. These other plants multiply while the areas of grass shrink. The animals find progressively less to eat while the harsh weeds that once were scarce replace the grasses until the latter are few and far apart.

To be successful under the climatic conditions of a desert, a plant must be well adapted either to avoid the prolonged droughts or to resist them. But about half of the kinds of vegetation in the desert are short-lived annuals. They remain dormant as seeds for decades if necessary, then germinate after a drenching rain, take root, produce a few leaves, send up flowers, and ripen their seeds in just a few weeks. By the time the desert is dry again, only those seeds survive to carry on the tradition. These plants are called "ephemeral" annuals since their growing season is so short and unpredictable.

The long-lived kinds of vegetation in the desert are mostly harsh shrubs or spiny succulents, such as the cacti. They have leaves that are highly adapted for holding back moisture while exchanging gases, or leaves only after a rain has stimulated new growth, or no leaves at all. Creosote bush retains its leathery leaves through the driest weather, but curls them until only the waxy upper surface is exposed and the hairs on the underside are all squeezed together. Sagebrush, which grows also on semiarid land, gets its gray-green color from the waterproof coating over its leaves, which are small and

Sagebrush

have few stomata through which moisture could be lost. Palo verde is a small tree with bright green bark, that produces leaves and flowers only after a rain. For the rest of the year, it carries on photosynthesis only in its bark. The many kinds of cacti produce leaves only for a short time while they are seedlings. Thereafter they have no foliage at any season, and depend upon photosynthesis in the green surface layers of their succulent stems. Mesquite and cottonwood trees are exceptional in having green leaves most of the year in warm deserts. But they survive only where their roots reach deeply into underground streams, often where water sinks into the stony beds of temporary rivers that are flooded for a few hours after each local rainstorm.

GREEN LIFE ON MOUNTAIN PEAKS AND POLAR LANDS

On many a high mountain slope and in polar lands as well, the growing season is longer and more regular each year than on any desert. It is longer, but more subject to harsh weather, than it is for spring wild flowers on the floor of a deciduous forest. Yet there are so many similarities between the climate at high altitudes and high latitudes that quite a number of the same or closely related plants live in both, and also as familiar forest wild flowers at low altitudes and modest latitudes.

The glacier lilies that raise their golden flowers at the 8,000-foot level and higher on the Rocky Mountains within a week after the winter snow melts and uncovers them belong to the same genus as the dogtooth violets of eastern woodlands. The goldthread that blossoms on the mountains of New England at elevations higher than trees will grow is the same one that lives in treeless Greenland and on the forest floor in temperate eastern North America. A closely related goldthread grows close to the snow line in our western mountains, and at lower elevations in the arctic portions of Alaska and northern Asia.

Both on high mountains and toward the North Polar regions, the vegetation shows a distinctive boundary caused by the harsh weather conditions. Known as the tree line (or timber line), it is the highest altitude or latitude at which the wind permits upright growth of trees. Along this line, the trees show a characteristically grotesque form. They are pruned by the winter gales, which snap off every twig that extends beyond the contour. The trees take on a permanent bend or twist that shows which direction the wind blows. No branches at all may grow on the upwind side because every bud there is killed by wind-driven sleet, hail and mineral particles too. In the Bavarian Alps, trees of this form are called Krummholz ("crooked wood").

Until recently, no one realized that the oldest living things are trees close to tree line in the White Mountains of eastern California. Despite the harsh weather, parts of these bristle-cone pines have continued to grow a little each summer for as many as 4,700 years. To keep pace with the rate of erosion which takes away fully an inch from the surface of the mountain each century, the surviving roots must extend downward an extra fraction of an inch each season. The living branches add to their length and produce another set of reproductive cones, just as they have been doing for millenia. Each branch retains its short needles for several years, and thereby earns the tree its other name of foxtail pine.

Woody skeletons of dead trees of the same kind still stand or lie on the stony ground at even higher elevations, showing that in the past the weather allowed this one type of vegetation to thrive farther from sea level than it does now.

Scientists who examine samples of the wood and then use computers to find the best match in the sequence of years with good growth and poor tell us that these skeletons record the effects of weather as much as 9,000 years into the past. That was right after the end of the last great Ice Age.

No comparable trees have been found yet in the arctic tundra to the north of the limit of the coniferous forests. There, as on the alpine tundra, the only trees are just a few inches high. They are birches and alders, with some spruces and firs. They grow mostly where rocky outcroppings shield the thin soil from the wind. Their roots are all extremely shallow, for the arctic tundra differs from its alpine counterpart in another way: only the top few inches of soil thaw in the low summer sun. Below this is frozen ground called permafrost, which has been there since the beginning of the Ice Age.

The permafrost prevents surface water from draining downward, and resists the formation of rivers. In consequence, wherever the land is fairly level in the arctic tundra, it accumulates pools of water from melted snow. Aquatic plants grow quickly in the long summer days. Waterfowl and shorebirds arrive by the million to nest around the pools and to eat either the plants or the small animals that are the first consumers. Peat moss rims many of the pools. Grasses and sedges are numerous, particularly the sedge called cotton grass. Its name comes from the tufts of long white silky bristles that make its clusters of flowers and fruits so conspicuous. On the ridges between one pool and the next, wild flowers and low shrubby plants find a place. Most of them are of the same kinds that live on alpine tundras farther south.

The land plants of Antarctica are far fewer. Only two kinds of grasses have been found there, and one kind of flowering plant. Mosses and lichens make up the remainder of the terrestrial vegetation. Too few pools form in the short summer to nourish migratory waterfowl—and none arrive. A few crustaceans and insects feed on the scattering of aquatic plants, all of which are algae. Yet in the past, Antarctica had much more vegetation. Seams of coal there reveal fossils representing land plants that flourished during the Age of Reptiles more than 65 million years ago. Possibly in the future, a change in the weather pattern of the world will again allow the continent around the South Pole to have greenery in profusion.

4

How Plants Live

When we think of van Helmont's famous willow tree, which grew from a weight of 5 pounds to 169 pounds in five years, we realize how different most plants are from most animals. The willow had no need to move from its pot, or make a sound. It spent no energy in waving its branches or capturing organic matter as food. Inconspicuously it absorbed water and mineral nutrients, carbon dioxide from the air, and light. From these simple ingredients it built roots, trunk, branches, leaves, flowers and fruits.

At 169 pounds, the willow was still a young tree. If given a chance, it would have continued to grow tall and spreading until it weighed many tons. If van Helmont had cut off almost any branch from his tree and thrust the severed end in a jar of water, it would have formed scar tissue and then put forth roots—these would have anchored the branch in the soil, absorbed mineral nutrients and water, and transformed the single branch into a whole new tree. Similar methods of propagation are customary in agricultural practice for culti-

vation of bananas, sugar cane, and several other crops. It is a
housewife's trick for "starting over" a geranium that has
grown too big and straggly, or for adding to the collection of
plants on the windowsill a coleas or an African violet with
attractive features, beginning with just a small piece from
another plant.

We are more likely to notice details of house plants that
we see many times each day from close range. If the leaves
sag a little, the plant probably is beginning to wilt because it
needs more water. If the leaves become yellowish green,
the problem may be a lack of some important mineral nutrient,
as a deficiency that can be corrected by adding a small amount
of fertilizer. If the stem grows long and spindly, the plant
may need more light than it is getting. Each symptom can be
a guide to improving the plant's environment toward supporting normal, healthy growth.

Good farmers watch their crops outdoors in the same critical
way, and take appropriate action when some abnormality is
detected. Yet to correctly interpret the appearance of the
plant as it changes through a year, a person needs to understand how the plant lives, what its needs are, and what to do
to help without harm. Too much fertilizer will kill almost
any plant. An excess of water is fatal to a cactus, and intense
sunlight disastrous to an African violet, a cacao tree, or a
tobacco plant.

Particularly in winter, it is often difficult to tell whether a
plant is still alive. So many of the processes of life are dormant
then that the distinction between a healthy plant and nonliving material seems slight. In a plant, we cannot look for
movement as a sign of life. Growth can be at a standstill, so
that absence of growth is no criterion by itself. Reproduction
is a capacity of all forms of life, but failure to reproduce does
not indicate death or that the material is nonliving. Irritability
is a characteristic of living things, and shown at appropriate
times in relation to changes in illumination, temperature,
pressure and similar stimuli. Yet a dry seed or an oak tree in
February is scarcely more irritable than a stone. Nor can we

base a sound judgment on the definite form and range in size that are distinguishing features of plants, rather than of nonliving things, for the dead body of a plant may still show the normal shape and dimensions. Chemical composition might be relied upon, for living things contain many very large molecules of proteins, carbohydrates and fats, whereas molecular sizes are usually small among substances that never have been part of living systems. But proteins, carbohydrates and fats are still a part of plants for weeks or months or years after life is gone. Cellular organization remains too, sometimes for millions of years in fossils, making it another unreliable criterion of life.

The only real clue to life as opposed to death is a continuous demand for energy. Even the dormant seed or the oak tree in February is absorbing oxygen, releasing carbon dioxide and heat—perhaps water too—at a slow, though measurable pace. The rate increases when the seed germinates or the tree puts out new buds. Then it follows a new pattern through the rest of the growing season because photosynthesis each day captures and stores energy beyond the immediate needs. Only in darkness does the green plant resume its ordinary respiration.

ABSORBING NOURISHMENT

For an aquatic plant, the environment affords an unlimited supply of water and usually a generous reserve of carbon dioxide for photosynthesis. Dissolved mineral matter, particularly phosphates and nitrates, may be critically low in concentration. And energy from the sun is available only to modest depths.

On land, where the solar energy is much more plentiful, water is often in short supply and dissolved mineral nutrients locally so scarce that they limit growth. Roots serve the plant well in probing through the soil into places where water and the necessary nutrients are likely to be.

The fundamental organization in a root provides simultaneously for absorption, anchorage, and continued growth.

All of these remarkable features can be visualized by examining through a hand lens the young roots that extend so quickly from a germinating radish seed. The details are especially visible if it is kept in a transparent container that maintains the necessary high humidity while the seed rests atop a small sheet of black paper on wet paper toweling.

Covering the slender tip of the root is a thimble-shaped mass of cells called the root cap. Ordinarily these cells are pushed ahead of the growing root between the particles of the soil, and protect the important growth center of the root from mechanical damage. From the growth center, new cells move out in four mainstreams. Some go into the root cap, to take the place of those that are worn away. The others become parts of the tissues in the root, with roles that contribute directly to the welfare of the rest of the plant. Some of these cells soon form a sheath, just one cell thick, comprising the delicate epidermis like a thin skin over the root. Others become a cylindrical mass of tissue at the center of the root, and serve there in rapid conduction of watery solutions to the stem and of elaborated foods to the root from the leaves. Between these conducting (or vascular) cells and the epidermis, the young root comes to contain a thick sheath of almost spherical cells loosely packed together; these form the layer called the cortex. Although so unimpressive in appearance, the cortex cells do much of the work of the root.

For a short distance back of the root tip with its root cap, the cells in all of these layers continue to elongate as well as divide, pushing the root forward. Then comes a region of slightly greater age—measured in hours, rather than in days or weeks. In it, elongation has ceased. There the epidermal cells begin to extend an obvious fuzz of fine root hairs. If surrounded by soil, these extensions would slide between the particles of mineral matter and greatly increase the surface through which the root could absorb moisture and dissolved nutrients. Yet the root-hair zone has a dynamic quality, for it is added to at the one end and disappears at the other where the root hairs shrivel and cease to function.

Until a few decades ago, not even the most knowledgeable scientists realized how rapidly and forcefully a plant takes in water and mineral nutrients. Without commotion it transfers these important materials through its root hairs toward the center of the root, through the rest of each epidermal cell, from one cell of the cortex to the next, and finally to the special nonliving cells of the wood for lengthwise passage to the rest of the plant. Experiments with half-inch lengths of root from tomato seedlings showed that in these small living organs of a plant that normally grows only a few feet tall is all the organization necessary to force watery solutions much higher than the top of the loftiest redwood tree.

High pressures due to work by cells in the cortex of the roots are needed most by trees that have shed all of their leaves in one season and until they expand their new foliage in the next season. Once their fresh leaves are functioning, a physical phenomenon takes over the work of rasing the watery solutions all the way from the roots. It requires no expenditure of energy, no matter how much water is moved.

The conducting tubes in the vascular cylinder at the center of the young roots are connected to others in the trunk and branches, all the way through the twigs and leaf stalks into the ultimate veinlets of the leaves. There the watery solutions pass from cell to cell, eventually to those where photosynthesis takes place. Among vascular plants, these are the cells that contain chloroplastids as microscopic inner structures (organelles). Chloroplastids get their name and color from the essential green pigment, chlorophyll, which occupies definite sites on internal membranes of exquisite thinness. There the water and dissolved carbon dioxide are used and oxygen released through complex reactions, whereby some of the energy of light is bound up into new molecules of organic compounds.

The rest of the water and essentially all of the oxygen that is the byproduct of photosynthesis leave the leaf through a seemingly haphazard system of air spaces between the cells that contain the chloroplastids. These spaces connect to the outside world through many narrow passageways, each flanked

by two special guard cells. Although the guard cells are part
of the epidermis of the leaf, they differ from other epidermal
cells in possessing chloroplastids. When photosynthesis is
possible, the guard cells manufacture organic compounds
and induce water to enter from all of the adjacent epidermal
cells by the physical process of osmosis. The extra water
inside the guard cells alters their shape. Like lips pursed into
the position for whistling, each pair of cells open the air space
between them. If a cloud passes over, they close the passage-
way a little. At night, or if the plant wilts a little, they shut it
altogether and conserve the moisture within the leaf. Actually, when all of these passageways (which are called stomata)
are open simultaneously, the outward diffusion of water vapor
and oxygen and the inward diffusion of carbon dioxide are
almost as rapid as though the leaf had no epidermis at all.

For many years, the obvious action of the guard cells and
the inability of the best compound microscopes to reveal inner
details of the leaf, combined to distract attention from a
process of at least equal value to the plant. With better instruments, scientists have now been able to examine the ultramicroscopic details where the air spaces come in contact with
the walls of the cells containing the chloroplastids. Like
essentially all cell walls within the plant, these are of cellulose
and form an inert, tough external skeleton around each cell.
Water diffuses readily through the living membrane of the cell
and moves through the meshwork of cellulose molecules in the
wall to form extremely small curved surfaces facing the air in
the intercellular spaces. The form and size of these surfaces
make them cling with amazing strength to the cellulose.
Through the curved surfaces, oxygen emerges from solution
and diffuses away while carbon dioxide dissolves and moves
inward, enters the cell and reaches the chloroplastids.

Equally important is the evaporation of water molecules
from the ultramicroscopic curved surfaces into the intercellular
spaces. As much as nine-tenths of the liquid that rises through
the conducting tubes of the stem leaves the plant by way of
the intercellular spaces and the stomata. But for every mole-

cule of water that evaporates in this way, another moves to
take its place. Water molecules hold tightly to others of their
own kind, forming unbroken threads far stronger than steel
wires of the same dimension. They extend all the way from the
cells that conduct photosynthesis in the leaf through its veins,
down the twigs and branches and trunk, to the ultimate root
hairs, and into the water films that coat the particles of soil.
Due to the evaporative discharge of water from the myriad
surfaces within each leaf—a process called evapotranspiration
—water molecules move against the force of gravity to the
topmost leaf without the plant expending energy in any way.

It is tempting to think of evapotranspiration as an un-
avoidable loss of water suffered while getting carbon dioxide
for photosynthesis and discharging waste oxygen. This inter-
pretation overlooks the role the transpired water has already
had inside the plant, transporting mineral nutrients in dilute
solution. Certainly too much water can be discharged when
sunlight causes guard cells to open the stomata during a time
of drought. But when the air is saturated with water vapor,
as it is just before dawn on many days in summer, the plant
still has need to move its water columns with their load of
nutrients. Evapotranspiration cannot provide the force. Root
pressure may not be needed. Instead, the leaves spend energy
in secreting excess water from the tips of the veins, by a process called guttation. Many of the sparkling droplets along
leaf edges at dawn originated in this way.

CAPTURING ENERGY

The most elusive feature of green plants is certainly their
utilization of simple raw materials and free energy from the
sun to produce organic compounds from which energy can
later be recovered for use. No other kinds of life possess this
secret. But although the search for an explanation has been
narrowed by the discovery that the whole operation is handled
neatly within each chloroplastid, the challenge and much of
the mystery remain.

Parts of the puzzle have been identified. In most plants, the light is absorbed by the chlorophyll, and the efficiency of photosynthesis is in proportion to the rate of absorption in each part of the solar spectrum. Chlorophyll is green in both reflected and transmitted light because it absorbs light nonuniformly—more in the orange and blue than in the green. But the pigment itself is not changed by the light. It merely becomes excited in a physical way, and passes along the energy it absorbs to other compounds within the chloroplastid. The consequences all hinge on the splitting of water molecules, releasing oxygen as a waste product and gaining both ionized hydrogen and electrons. Some of the energy in the electrons is used to reclaim the chlorophyll and make it ready to usefully absorb more light. Some is lost as heat. The rest, along with the hydrogen-ions, take part in the reactions whereby carbon dioxide is captured and combined with the hydrogen to make organic matter.

Chemists once believed that, if only their tests could be made delicate enough, they would find the hydrogen from the water incorporated with the carbon and oxygen from carbon dioxide to produce the simplest of all carbohydrates—formaldehyde (CH_2O). They realized that, except at minute concentrations, this is a poisonous material. But they thought it could be quickly made harmless by joining many molecules together, such as six at a time to form grape sugar (glucose, $C_6H_{12}O_6$) or five at a time to produce the less common carbohydrate arabinose ($C_5H_{10}O_5$). But careful studies have shown a far more roundabout sequence of chemical reactions yielding no formaldehyde and no single carbohydrate as "the" product in photosynthesis.

Carbohydrates comprise a whole family of organic compounds, composed solely of carbon, hydrogen and oxygen, with half as many oxygen atoms as hydrogen atoms—just as in water (H_2O). Cane sugar (sucrose, $C_{12}H_{22}O_{11}$) meets these requirements, and so do the larger molecules of starch, cellulose and lignin. All of these the green plant can synthesize, and then digest again if need be.

By molecular rearrangements, the proportion of oxygen in

organic molecules can be reduced, yielding the various compounds that chemists call lipids, which include oils, fats and waxes. These too can be digested later and their chemical binding energy released for life processes. Most of them consist of long chains called fatty acids, linked in threes to the triple alcohol known as glycerine or glycerol.

The largest molecules in which the green plant stores some of the energy it captures from the sun are proteins, each composed of units called amino acids linked together in a characteristic way. To make proteins, the plant must have nitrogen in the form of nitrates or nitrites among the mineral nutrients from the soil. A few, such as rice, seem able to get along with nitrogen from ammonia. Some others, most notably the members of the legume family (such as clover and alfalfa), possess on their roots special enlargements (nodules) in which microbes produce the nitrogen-containing compounds from gaseous nitrogen taken from air in the soil. Proteins in the living cell have special roles in expediting chemical reactions that otherwise would progress too slowly to be useful. These materials also link up with lipids to form the many living membranes on which the chemical activities take place. Generally proteins are too important to life to be used for food by plants except in dire emergency. More often, they are disassembled into their component amino acids and resynthesized into new forms, for the variety of proteins is almost endless.

Much of the guidance that underlies the chemical operations of living cells is inherited and released throughout the scene of activity by molecules of still another category—the nucleotides. They join together with links of 5-carbon sugar and phosphate to form nucleic acids such as those that carry the genetic code (DNA, or deoxyribose nucleic acid) or serve in its transcription (RNA, or ribonucleic acid). The simpler nucleotides are even more active, transferring energy from one compound to another, mostly through the agency of one called ATP (adenosine triphosphate).

Uniquely, the chemistry of life makes use of ATP to combine two reactions and obtain a product containing more energy than any of the raw materials. At first, this seemed to disprove the respected Second Law of Thermodynamics which states that some energy must be lost in heat when a transfer of any kind takes place. But a living cell, by losing a little heat in each of two transfers, manages to salvage a little too and incorporate it in a bigger molecule than either of the two that were combined. For example, glucose (grape sugar) and fructose (fruit sugar) are both carbohydrates with six carbon atoms per molecule. By these two characteristic steps, they can be combined to form sucrose (cane sugar or beet sugar), a carbohydrate with twelve carbon atoms in each molecule. The energy for this combination comes from ATP, which is degraded to ADP (adenosine diphosphate) and free phosphate. The molecular biologist might represent these two reactions most simply as

$$(1) \quad \text{glucose} + \text{ATP} \xrightarrow[\text{appropriate protein}]{\text{in the presence of the}} \text{glucose-phosphate} + \text{ADP}$$
$$+ \text{ heat}$$

$$(2) \quad \text{glucose-phosphate} + \text{fructose} \xrightarrow[\text{different protein}]{\text{in the presence of a}} \text{sucrose}$$
$$+ \text{ phosphate} + \text{heat}$$

Later, for other uses (such as respiration), either a plant and an animal can digest the sucrose by still another reaction that releases heat—and hence will proceed spontaneously as soon as the appropriate protein is added to facilitate the reaction:

$$(3) \quad \text{sucrose} + \text{water} \xrightarrow[\text{protein called sucrase}]{\text{in the presence of the}} \text{glucose} + \text{fructose}$$
$$+ \text{ heat}$$

Thus all of the reactions in molecular biology follow the Second Law of Thermodynamics. By capturing and transferring energy in countless ways, always losing some as heat, they make life possible and give it an indefinite future.

DISTRIBUTING MATERIALS

The most obvious product of photosynthesis is starch, which is stored temporarily in the cells where the solar energy is captured. Adjacent, colorless cells of a leaf that is mottled in green and white receive enough nourishment to stay alive, but no surplus to store. A simple experiment confirms this: the variegated leaf is killed by immersing it for 30 seconds in boiling water, then extracted of its chlorophyll with hot 70 percent alcohol, and finally stained with a strong solution of iodine* which colors the starch dark blue. If part of the leaf has been kept shaded with a patch of black cloth that lets carbon dioxide through but blocks the light, this area too will show no evidence of starch.

At night, the cells of the leaf digest their starch, converting them to sugars and sending them to other parts of the plant by way of conducting tubes within the veins and the vascular cylinder of the twigs, branches, trunk and roots. These same conducting tubes convey amino acids, fatty acids and glycerol, which can be utilized to build proteins and lipids or stored elsewhere to match the needs of the plant.

The cells through which these organic compounds are distributed are called sieve cells or sieve tubes because their end walls are perforated and the living protoplasm of one cell is in obvious contact with that of the next. This makes easier the transfer of large molecules under complete control. The sieve cells or sieve tubes ordinarily are located in the upper part of each vein and the outer part of the vascular cylinder. In most trees they are components of the inner bark. When a maple tree is tapped in early spring to collect sweet sap toward the preparation of maple syrup, the collecting spile is driven in only to reach these cells of the inner bark. The scientific name chosen by botanists for the tissue in which the organic materials are transported is simply the Greek word for bark (phloem—pronounced "flow'-em").

* A small amount of potassium iodide should be added to make the iodine soluble.

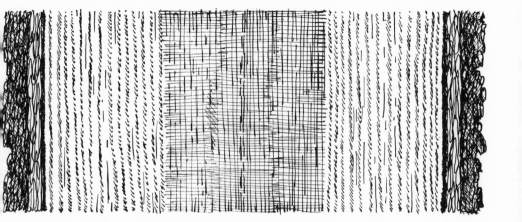

From bark to bark through sapwood and heartwood

If the spile is driven into the maple tree more deeply, it reaches the sapwood in which only the watery solutions of inorganic nutrients are being transported. These conducting cells are almost all dead and otherwise empty. The dilute solutions flow through them because of the pumplike action of root pressure or the capillary action due to transpiration pull in the leaves. The cells through which the water moves are located in the lower part of each vein and the center of the vascular cylinder in stem and root. Those that are still in use comprise the sapwood of a tree trunk. Others, which have been retired from service, remain as the heartwood. All of these tubular cells are reinforced by special thickening in their walls, resisting both internal pressure that might otherwise cause them to burst and also reduced pressure that could otherwise cause collapse. The tissue in which these water-conducting cells have a place is known by the Greek word for wood (xylem—pronounced "zi'-lem"). Its strength makes it a favorite construction material, while the stored energy that holds together its molecules (particularly of cellulose) gives it great value as fuel.

GROWING BIGGER

Most land plants possess growth centers in addition to those near the tip of the root and in the bud at the end of the stem. Ordinarily the root has a way of branching. The bud on the stem produces not only leaves and more stem but also the special lateral buds from which side branches will develop. In temperate and polar lands, where the terminal bud is protected all winter by special waterproof leaves called bud scales, the extent of new growth can usually be discovered by looking for the successive rings of scars where the scales fell off in early spring. In a good year, with plenty of water as well as warm weather and sunshine, an oak stem may add four inches or more to its length, whereas a poor year is shown by an addition of an inch or less.

The diameter of the stem and root can be increased too if the plant develops a growth center in the form of a thin sheath of cells called the vascular cambium, between the phloem and the xylem. From the cambium, more conducting tubes are formed to serve an increasing number of roots and leaves as the plant grows.

The new xylem cells are added in concentric sheaths as sapwood spreading radially outward from the old xylem. Progressively this enlarges the woody part of the plant. But the faster growth that takes place during wet portions of the growing season is accomplished by adding xylem tubes of larger diameter rather than by increasing the rate of addition. As the weather turns drier, the cambium adds xylem tubes of smaller size. Consequently, in parts of the world where rains are more frequent in spring than in summer, the new spring wood is conspicuously coarser than the new summer wood. The change between the last new xylem cells added in late summer or autumn and those produced the following spring may be so abrupt that, in a cross section of a stem or tree

trunk, it is easy to count the "annual rings" of alternating
pale spring sapwood and dark summer wood. If the dark
rings are counted all the way from the outermost wood to
the center of the tree, the age of the tree at that particular
level can be learned. To get this information without killing
the tree, a tool called an increment borer is used. It is a
cylindrical auger with a spiral ridge at the end, which draws
it into the wood when rotated; the hollow center of the tool
protects a cylindrical sample of the wood as a "core" in which
the alternating pale and dark bands can be examined. Scientists who use this method to learn from the growth of old trees
the sequence of wet years and dry ones far into the past call
themselves dendrochronologists.

As the vascular cambium adds new xylem and enlarges the
woody part of a plant, it also adds new phloem where it is in
contact with the older phloem. This addition is less spectacu-

Growth record in a cut tree trunk

lar since the size of the new phloem cells does not vary
greatly and their walls are relatively thin. Phloem tissue gets
its strength from special cells of a different type, called fibers,
which tend to be mixed in among the conducting cells. Each
fiber begins as a long slender cell containing living protoplasm. As it matures, however, the protoplasm secretes cellulose toughened by lignin on the inside of the original wall
until almost no space remains at the center. Unable to get
nourishment through the thick wall, the protoplasm dies,
leaving the dead fiber to resist lengthwise strains in the inner
bark and protect the vital conducting cells there.

The outer bark is composed of waterproof, corky cells that
are produced by thin, overlapping patches of cork cambium
just outside the inner bark. They arise in the cortex layer of
each young stem as soon as growth of the vascular cylinder
threatens to rupture the original thin epidermis. The plant
keeps its living cells covered by dead ones in this way, almost
completely preventing loss of moisture through the bark. It
also shuts out many insects, fungi and bacteria that would
otherwise invade it.

The softest and most nutritious cells in a tree are the conducting tubes of the inner bark and the thin sheath of vascular cambium. If a bark beetle or a fungus can gain access to
this region, its food supply is assured. But if many beetles
tunnel there or the fungus strands destroy the cambium and
the phloem tubes, the plant soon dies. Its roots starve first.
Its growth ceases promptly. These same consequences follow
removal of the bark down to the delicate vascular cambium.
Just one narrow band of destruction, such as might be made
with a sharp saw, will "girdle" a tree and kill it if continued
completely around. Primitive man killed trees deliberately to
increase his supply of dry wood as fuel or to expose the soft
rich soil as a place for crops; he merely pounded with a stone
against the bark on all sides until every conducting tube and
cambium cell had been crushed. He did not know what he
was doing—merely that the method worked. Now we can
understand the vulnerability of a growing tree.

KEEPING COORDINATED

Among the organic substances distributed through phloem cells are several different kinds called plant hormones ("phytohormones"). They serve as chemical messengers, stimulating growth or elongation of cells or inhibiting these actions. Most of these special substances are synthesized in leaves or in the buds at the end of stems. Their effects are noticeable in other organs of the plant, and account for many changes resembling those that an animal would accomplish through use of its sense organs, nervous system and muscles. With its hormones and lacking these other special structures, a plant keeps coordinated remarkably well.

The first plant hormone to be identified proved to be a relatively simple compound known to chemists as indole, 3-acetic acid. Its common name is auxin, a word derived from the Greek equivalent of the verb to grow. It is a growth hormone in the sense that it stimulates elongation of young stem cells, inhibits the development of lateral buds, and restrains the elongation of young root cells. Auxin is destroyed by strong light, and influenced in its distribution by gravity, which tends to concentrate the hormone in the lower half of horizontal stems or roots. These features of the plant hormone account for the turning of stems toward light, of roots away from light, of stems away from the earth, of roots toward the earth, as well as the greater elongation of both roots and stems in dim light, and the delay that is customary before the side branches on a stem develop.

If an ordinary plant, such as a potted geranium, is turned on its side and kept in the dark for a few days, the auxin from the stem tip stimulates elongation of cells in the lower part of the stem but not in the upper part. The unequal rates of elongation cause the stem tip to be turned upward, away from the earth. Inside the pot and hidden from view, the auxin is similarly more concentrated in the lower half of the root and inhibits it from elongating. The upper half, without this restraint, does elongate, turning the root downward toward the earth.

If the same plant had been placed upright where it received all of its light from one side, the elongation of its stem would have been greatest in the direction of shade. This unequal rate of elongation turns the stem tip toward the light. If the roots were exposed and similarly illuminated from one side, the destruction of auxin on the lighted side would permit elongation there to be faster than on the shaded side, turning the root tip away from the light. A plant whose stem is intensely illuminated from all sides has so much of its auxin destroyed that it elongates very slowly and is said to be "low-growing." Without auxin to inhibit the development of its side branches, they begin growing, making the plant shrubby. Housewives often accomplish the same effect by pinching off the terminal bud, which is the principal source of auxin in the stem.

Each leaf produces some auxin and transfers it to the stem, increasing the concentration there and contributing to the inhibitory effect on side branches in the vicinity. But as a leaf ages, its production of auxin diminishes. Apparently the leaf stalk is sensitive to the change. As soon as the principal movement of auxin is from the stem into the leaf, the leaf stalk develops a crosswise disk of dead corky cells where it joins the stem. Eventually only the conducting cells of the xylem and phloem remain in operation. A strong wind can snap them off and tear the leaf free. On the stem a scar remains, marking the area where the leaf was formerly attached. Often it shows tiny dots where the vascular strands finally broke and were quickly closed, preventing loss of anything from the stem and deterring invasion by any foreign kinds of life. A similar mechanism controls the dropping of fruits, which also produce auxin so long as they are green and carrying on photosynthesis.

Additional hormones control flowering, and other phenomena peculiar to plants, such as the dormancy of seeds. Poinsettia plants, which are native to tropical Mexico, are extremely sensitive to changes in the length of night and flower when night is longest—around Christmas time. If a bright

Poinsettia flowers surrounded
by red display leaves

light shines on them for a minute or so in the middle of every night, they fail to flower because their hormonal system has been upset. A period of exposure to cold weather is essential to many kinds of seeds and winter buds, toward making the cells that produce their hormones respond to warmth and moisture. Ordinarily this prevents a seed or a perennial plant from putting forth leaves during an unseasonably warm, wet period in late autumn, only to have the new growth killed by frost soon afterward.

DISPOSING OF WASTES

Unlike an animal that absorbs many organic compounds and inorganic substances for which it has no need, a plant is highly selective from among the nutrient substances available. This relieves it to a major extent from a need to dispose of conspicuous wastes. Yet in the course of living, it may accumulate some materials for which it seems to have no direct use. They can be found as inert resins in the heartwood of a tree, or crystals of calcium oxalate in leaves. The autumn colors that we find so beautiful in the foliage of some deciduous trees just before it drops off appear to have no real role. Some, particularly the yellows, are pigments that helped in the capture of light and remain, exposed, when the green chlorophyll is withdrawn. Others, especially the reds and purples, may be no more than colorful products of early degeneration.

In a sense, the fallen petal is like the fallen leaf and the dead branch that broke off partway up the trunk of a tall tree. They have all served the plant, and been expended. They are wastes, which decomposers can utilize while returning the mineral nutrients to the soil. Few animals can get nourishment from their wastes in a comparable way.

A great many substances that plants synthesize have long been classed as "secondary" because they serve no direct role in normal growth and reproduction. Yet indirectly, these materials may greatly benefit the plant. The sugary solutions and fragrant oils exuded by special glands in flowers represent an expenditure of resources, and a complete waste if no pollinating animals come along. The production of stiff, sharp spines and thorns gains the plant nothing, so far as is known, unless herbivores are prevented from biting the live leaves and stems. Sticky resins in special resin canals within the bark and leaves of coniferous trees seem valuable to the plant only when they repel hungry animals or mire insects that are trying to bore through to the nutritious phloem and cambium. Poisonous substances and antibiotic compounds in plants represent a similar diversion of raw materials and energy without gain unless they stop attackers from doing damage.

Clearly, each adaptive feature of a plant relates to the laws of chance. Spiny shrubs and trees are scarce in Australia, where large herbivorous animals are principally the big kangaroos that graze on local grasses. Plants that tolerate rapid chilling are numerous on alpine meadows and arctic tundras, but rare in the warm tropics. Plants that attract insects, birds and bats to their flowers grow at all levels in the tropical rain forests, and benefit from cross-pollination with a minimum production of pollen. By contrast, the northern conifers depend almost entirely upon wind pollination and waste vast quantities of this golden dust, so rich in oils and proteins. On the arctic tundras, most of the low plants propagate themselves vegetatively and frequently lose in a gamble with the weather because, when they do form flowers, cold and high winds so often keep grounded the few kinds of insects that might visit. So long as chance allows gains to outweigh the costs of waste, the plants continue their many patterns of life.

5

How Plants Reproduce

Although obtaining energy and using it to stay alive is certainly the first goal in all kinds of living things, spending some energy on reproduction is as clearly a second goal. The inevitability of death makes reproduction essential for perpetuation of the species. Chance seems to favor plants that, when barely mature, begin processes that yield new individuals, ensuring that younger members of the same kind will be alive in future years.

A great many special features have adaptive value in promoting success in reproduction. Yet the variations center around a fairly small number of common themes. Fundamentals of reproduction show fewer changes to match details of the environment than are to be found in roots, stems and leaves. For this reason, scientists rely upon similarities in reproduction to group together plants with ancestors in common.

Unlike most animals, plants quite commonly reproduce vegetatively. This is a sexless or asexual method, preceded by no joining together of special cells. Many plants reproduce sexually as well as asexually, although at different times and under more special conditions. Those that do show sexual reproduction can be arranged in a series beginning with plants whose reproductive cells are so alike (except in behavior) as to be indistinguishable, and ending with the flowering plants in which the egg cell and the representative of the sperm cell are so peculiar that they remained unrecognized until 1849. To a self-taught botanist just twenty-six years old, Wilhelm Hofmeister of Leipzig, belongs the credit for discovering the elusive details and for then describing them in his report, "On the Embryology of Flowering Plants." Two years later, in 1851, his second publication drew attention to a comparable pattern in the reproduction of bryophytes and of those vascular plants that produce no seeds—the ferns and horsetails and clubmosses. The phenomenon he drew to the attention of botanists everywhere is now known as alternation of generations. It has no counterpart among animals, but has a place in the lives of many thallophytes.

Still more conservative are the molecular patterns carried by the chromosomes, which participate in both asexual and sexual reproduction and sustain the inheritable features of each kind of life. These patterns appear in giant trees that live for millennia, in weeds that survive only a single season, in single-celled algae of many kinds, in coarse kelps, and in animals too. They are parts of the heritage from perhaps more than a billion years ago. How they are parcelled out in reproduction determines to a large extent how much variation develops among the offspring.

ASEXUAL REPRODUCTION

Until slightly more than a decade ago, the rapid pace at which bacterial cells can divide—one to become two, the two to become four, and so on—could be attributed to their simplicity of structure. Inside the microscopic cell, the inheritable features seemed scattered rather than in chromosomes of a distinct nucleus. With no chromosomes to be replicated and then separated into the two daughter cells, bacteria appeared simply to undergo crosswise division, which is a phenomenon called binary fission.

Improved techniques revealed that a bacterium has a single long chromosome in the form of a loop, as much as 900 times longer than the cell within which it lies folded repeatedly, back and forth. During the half hour or so between one division and the next, a replica of this chromosome must be spun off, ready to move into one daughter cell when the moment comes. At the same time, the parent cell must be frantically transcribing the inherited instructions and following them in getting nourishment, attending to respiration and probably excretion, synthesizing new molecules and fitting them into the cell membrane, the replica chromosome, and all of the other features that are characteristic of the living cell. Any mistake could be fatal. No one knows how many bacteria make mistakes and die, for they are too small to recognize as individuals and the ones that reproduce successfully too numerous for a few to be missed.

The filamentous green algae, such as pond scum, seem far less hurried and more informal in their asexual reproduction. Progressively each filament elongates as its cylindrical cells lengthen and then divide. Eventually the filament breaks, perhaps where one cell has died and decomposed. The two individuals produced by fragmentation of the parent are seldom of equal length, but each one continues to grow as the parent did.

A land plant, such as a moss or liverwort or grass, appears still more casual about asexual reproduction. It branches, always with new growth at the tips. Old parts die and decompose, leaving the branches unconnected, independent, as individuals. A great many plants with fibrous roots can similarly be divided deliberately, letting each piece from the original clump continue growing without relation to any other.

"One becomes two" has long been the description of asexual reproduction, to contrast it with two parents being needed to produce each offspring by sexual means. But in asexual reproduction, a single parent often produces many young at the same time. A bacterium or an alga can undergo multiple fission and free a dozen or more tiny individuals from each cell. Similarly, plants of far greater complexity can produce several new individuals simultaneously. Strawberry plants and hawkweeds send out horizontal stems in different directions, each stem tipped by a bud from which the foliage of a new plant expands while adventitious roots take a hold upon the soil. Tulip bulbs branch and become clusters, the new small bulbs beside the parent. If separated, each continues growth on its own.

Seedless plants, such as bananas and some types of cultivated orange and grapefruit, can be propagated only by asexual means. Horticultural varieties of roses and apples cannot produce seeds that grow into plants with the same desirable characteristics; they are perpetuated by the horticultural technique of grafting suitable branches onto the rooted stem of a sturdy, less valuable relative. Sugar cane and potatoes are grown from short lengths of stem, which put forth new roots and tops. In all of these procedures, the inherited features show no change. The new individuals are as alike as identical twins, and identical to the parent too. This is the benefit and the hazard in asexual reproduction. It provides new lives that are neither worse nor better fitted to the conditions of the environment, and with no flexibility to meet a change.

THE IMPORTANCE OF SEX

Ever since the importance of chromosomes in carrying the inheritable features of life was recognized early in the present century, two events in sexual reproduction have been appreciated for their contribution to variability among the offspring. The first comes when a sex cell from one parent adds its chromosomes to those of the sex cell from the other parent. In this step, two unlike lines of inheritance are combined, ensuring that the new individual will be slightly different from either parent. The differences may be of no consequence. Or, in a changing environment, they may spell success in some way for which neither parent was fitted.

The second event is a necessary sequel to the first if the number of chromosomes is to be kept constant. Ordinarily, this is a fixed feature for each kind of plant. If a sex cell with one complete set of chromosomes is to join with another sex cell with a second complete set of chromosomes, the product will be a cell with two sets of chromosomes combined—a double set. Before the new individual that develops from the cell with the double set of chromosomes reaches the stage of producing sex cells, the number must be halved. The halving process is found in all living things that reproduce by sexual means, and is called reduction division or meiosis (from the Greek equivalent for the verb to diminish). During meiosis, the double set of chromosomes go through a microscopic ballet in which the rules of chance provide random combinations of maternal and paternal chromosomes in the daughter cells.

Unlike animals, whose cells undergo the reduction division during formation of the eggs or sperms, plants produce their sex cells by ordinary cell division. Meticulously they replicate each chromosome and provide each daughter cell with an unchanged number of chromosomes. The reduction division in plants that reproduce sexually occurs, instead, when spores are being produced. Hence each spore ordinarily has the single number of chromosomes. In a canna or a crocus it is 3, in a trillium 6, in a sweet pea or a garden pea 7, in sweet clover or an onion 8, in ordinary cabbage or maize or milkweed 10, in Easter lilies or oaks or pines or tomatoes 12, and so on. The canna spore has three different chromosomes, each carrying its own portion of the plant's inheritance. The canna chromosomes are unlike those of the crocus in the features that are inherited, which is the reason that a canna differs from a crocus, despite the fact that both have three chromosomes in each spore.

ALTERNATION OF GENERATIONS

Unlike animals, the spore of a plant with sexual reproduction germinates or grows into an individual that produces sex cells, but not spores. The general word for a sex cell, without specifying whether it is an egg or a sperm, is a gamete. The plant that produces sex cells is a gamete-plant, or gametophyte. The growth of the gametophyte is entirely by ordinary cell division, which gives every cell the same number of chromosomes as the spore from which it grew—a single set. The gametes have this same chromosome number.

The word zygote is used for the cell produced by fusion of two gametes; it possesses the double set of chromosomes. In many kinds of plants, the zygote grows by ordinary cell division, which replicates the double set just as meticulously as it would one. A new individual can mature, each cell containing the double set of chromosomes. This is the spore-producing plant, called a sporophyte. Only a sporophyte ever develops roots, stems, leaves, cones or flowers.

In all plants that reproduce sexually, it is possible to identify a gametophyte generation and the gametes it produces, then the fusion of gametes (called fertilization) to form a zygote, and at least this one cell with the double set of chromosomes to represent the sporophyte generation. Among ferns, horsetails, clubmosses and all kinds of seed plants, the sporophyte is the conspicuous generation—the one we see. Inconspicuously these sporophytes produce spores by reduction division, and from these the gametophyte develops. This alternation of generations, from gametophyte to sporophyte and sporophyte to gametophyte, is the fundamental phenomenon among plants that Wilhelm Hofmeister discovered, earning himself a reputation as one of the great botanists of all time.

When we examine a filament of pond scum under the microscope, we see a gametophyte. The common kind, called *Spirogyra* because its chloroplastids are ribbon-shaped and spiral around just inside the cylindrical transparent wall of each cell, becomes sexually active in midsummer. Where filaments lie parallel close together, each cell may develop a rounded projection toward the adjacent filament. The projections join in pairs and open to form a tube. The contents of one cell round up and move through the tube to fuse with the contents of the adjacent cell. The one that moves is called the male gamete, and the other a female. But a single filament may show in this way that some of its cells are female and others male; apparently the difference in sex is minimal, although the fusing of the two nuclei and combination of two lines of inheritance is real. The zygote develops a heavy wall, and can survive drought and frost that would kill the ordinary cells of the filament. The zygote is also the only representative of the sporophyte generation for, under suitable circumstances, it undergoes reduction division and produces four spores, each with a single set of chromosomes. Of these spores, three are wasted while the fourth grows by ordinary cell division into a new filament—a new gametophyte.

The familiar moss plant is a gametophyte. In season, it forms at the top of its upright branches small multicellular sex organs. These are either flask-shaped and contain a single egg cell, or knoblike and filled with sperm cells. In moisture from dew or gentle rain, the sperm cells can swim to reach egg cells and fertilize them, producing zygotes. By special embryonic stages, the zygote grows to become a vertical stalk topped by an elaborate spore case. At first it is green and makes some of its own food. But for mineral nutrients and most of its water, it draws upon the green moss plant—the gametophyte branch that produced the egg cell. The slender stalk and spore case constitute the complete sporophyte. Within the spore case, by reduction division, spores are produced, each with a single set of chromosomes. After wind distributes the spores, those that fall in suitable environments germinate into new gametophytes. These branch and become the moss plants we see.

In most ferns, the spores are produced in minute spore cases grouped in "fruit dots" below the leaves. Each spore case ripens to become a slingshot that throws its spores vigorously into the breeze for dispersal. On suitable surfaces, such as the side of a wet flowerpot in a humid greenhouse or damp soil in a woodland, the spores germinate into small flat gametophytes less than half an inch across. Sex organs are pro-

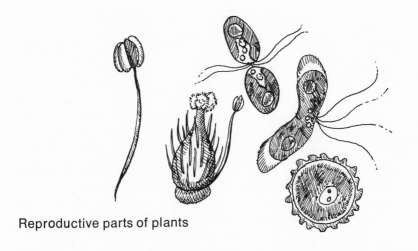

Reproductive parts of plants

duced and, with moisture, the sperms swim about and fertilize the egg cells. A single zygote from each gametophyte can grow to become the recognizable fern—a sporophyte. Both sporophyte and gametophyte are independent plants, but the one becomes much bigger than the other.

SPORES AND SEEDS

In a seed plant, the gametophytes are so small that they are hard to find. The male gametophytes, which produce male gametes (sperm cells), differ completely in origin, location and form from the female gametophytes, which produce egg cells (female gametes). Until Wilhelm Hofmeister made his discoveries, no one realized that the pollen sacs in which pollen develops are spore cases and the pollen grains are spores. These spores originated by reduction division in pollen sacs, such as those a pine tree bears on the scale-shaped parts of its pollen-producing cones. A flowering plant bears them as the enlarged tips of its stamens. In either case, the male gametophyte consists of only a few cells. They develop inside the pollen grain before and after the pollen is dispersed.

The spore case within which a female gametophyte develops in a seed-producing pine cone is a thin-walled sac, one of a pair attached to the upper surface of each cone scale. Inside the sac is a single large cell, which undergoes reduction division to yield four spores, only one of which develops further. It becomes a female gametophyte without separating from the tree that bore it. If moisture between the cone scales captures a pollen grain and, upon drying, pulls the grain close to the female gametophyte, the event of pollination may be followed by fertilization. First the male gametophyte must extend from the pollen grain a fine projection called a pollen tube. If the tip of this delicate tube, which contains two minute sperm cells, comes in contact with an egg cell produced by the female gametophyte, the tube wall dissolves and lets the gametes come together. In a white pine, about a year elapses between pollination and fertilization. Nearly another year is needed for the zygote to develop through its embryonic stages and reach a state of ripeness and dormancy. By then the pine cone has turned to hang downward. It dries out, separating its scales and letting the seeds drop into the wind. Each seed bears a thin wing from the surface of the cone scale, a thin seed coat derived from the spore case, and contains an embryo perhaps a quarter of an inch long, with a few tiny needles and very short new root.

The female gametophytes in a flowering plant are still more enclosed and protected. Those in a freshly opened tulip can be exposed by slicing lengthwise through the central pistil from its pollen-collecting tip to the stalk that supports the flower. Within the pistil are three chambers, each with two lengthwise lines of small knobs. Each knob is a spore case, known more commonly as an ovule. Within it, a single large cell undergoes reduction division to yield four spores, three of which shrivel while the fourth develops as the female gametophyte. To the end cell of the gametophyte, which is the single egg cell, a pollen tube may come, bringing close two minute sperm cells. In some flowers, the tube can grow this half inch or more in about fifteen minutes; in others, it takes a month. But instead of wasting one sperm cell while the other fuses with the egg (as in the pine and other gymnosperms), the flowering plant accomplishes a unique double fertilization.

One sperm cell joins with the egg cell to produce a zygote, from which the embryo will grow. The nucleus from the other sperm cell fuses with two or more nuclei of the female gametophyte and initiates the growth of a peculiar tissue called the endosperm. Endosperm becomes a source of nourishment for the embryo either before the seed is ripe or later while it is germinating.

PROVISION FOR THE YOUNG

The embryo in the seed of each flowering plant is wrapped in the seed coat derived from the spore case (ovule) wall, and also by the wall of the ovary in which the ovules were all concealed. These are parts of the preceding sporophyte generation, now surrounding the new sporophyte plant. The ovary wall, plus any adhering parts of the flower, constitutes a fruit enclosing the seeds. It is an extra covering, which a pine seed lacks, and often helps the plant to get its seeds dispersed. Botanists regard the ovary wall as so important that they use it in distinguishing between the angiosperms (from the Greek *angeion* = a container or covering) and gymnosperms (from the Greek *gymnos* = naked, and *spermos* = a seed). Physically it is a small difference, yet one with an ancient history of great significance. Flowering plants (angiosperms) have fruits; gymnosperms do not.

The source of nourishment for the young seedling is always the mature plant of the preceding sporophyte generation. But its storage site next to the embryo differs greatly in the various kinds of seed plants. In a pine seed, it is in tissue remaining from the female gametophyte, hence in cells whose nuclei have a single set of chromosomes. Among angiosperms, the female gametophyte is totally obliterated by the developing endosperm, but the latter varies too in its permanence.

A corn kernel is actually a fruit, in which the ovary wall and the seed coat have joined, as is customary among cereal grasses. The embryo is visible as a small, white, oval or lens-shaped part near the point of attachment to the corn cob, on the upper surface of the kernel. Everything else inside the seed coat is endosperm, the nuclei of which have at least three sets of chromosomes. All of this tissue is digested and absorbed by the young seedling when it germinates.

A whole peanut is also a fruit, with a thin, irregular, pale ovary wall and usually two or more seeds inside. Each seed has its own wrapper, as a reddish brown seed coat as thin as tissue paper. But before the seeds ripen, all of the nourishment that once was in the endosperm is transferred into the first pair of seed leaves, which are called cotyledons. They are parts of the embryo, which has a double set of chromosomes in each nucleus. It was dormant and alive until it was boiled or roasted.

Living slowly on its food reserves, the embryo in a seed waits for conditions of moisture and temperature to become suitable for growth. If these conditions are not supplied, the number of surviving seeds diminishes. After ten years, few remain alive. Sometimes those that could still germinate have such dry, hard seed coats that no moisture can penetrate to awaken the embryo. Agriculturalists can often increase the proportion of seeds that will germinate by putting them in a machine that scratches almost through the seed coat and lets water in more easily. The record is still held by some large lotus seeds that remained dormant for more than 100 years, then produced normal plants when botanists cut through the hard seed coats with a file and soaked the seeds in lukewarm water.

In a few kinds of plants, the connection between a seed and the stalk on which it grew does not break until after germination has progressed a while. On mangrove trees along muddy seashores and brackish rivers in the tropics, the seedling has a long dagger-shaped root and a few green leaves before it breaks away. Then it drops so quickly that the root may be thrust several inches into the mud and is held securely. If the tide happens to be high when the mangrove seedling falls, it splashes and then floats away, perhaps to be left elsewhere on the mudflat where it can stay and grow to become a tree.

In the deserts of the American Southwest, some of the century plants retain their seedlings high on the towering spire of the floral cluster. The mature plant transfers the last of its water into the several two-inch leaves of the seedlings and then dies. The young plants eventually drop off, and may be blown by strong wind along the ground for many yards. Each seedling continues daily with photosynthesis at a low rate, month after month using up the reserve of moisture in its thick, succulent leaves. In this way it may survive until a rainstorm comes and soaks the ground. With added moisture, it can quickly root itself and grow.

6
How Plants Inherit

For years, people have said, "Like begets like." And a few have added, "but not quite." If half a dozen dry seeds from the same seed pod of a garden pea plant are tucked into well-mixed soil in a pan and kept uniformly moist and at moderate temperature, they do not all send up seedlings in the same hour, or produce little plants as alike as though they had been manufactured by a machine. They are "not quite" alike. But certainly they are all pea plants and not oak trees or sea-weeds.

In neither plants nor animals was this mechanism widely understood until during the present century. Back in 1865, an observant monk presented to the scientific world a published report that told how certain features of pea plants were inherited in his garden. But the laws of inheritance offered by this pioneering man, Gregor Johann Mendel, matched no information known to the scientists of his day. Neglected, they were set aside until 1900, when three independent biologists rediscovered them and confirmed their importance.

One of Mendel's accomplishments showed him to be ahead of his time. He isolated 14 different characteristics among the pea plants he was raising and found that they bred true when particular plants were self-pollinated. In this technique, he excluded insects by covering with little cloth bags all of the flowers on each experimental plant; then he used a soft brush to transfer pollen from the stamens of one flower to the sticky tip (the stigma) of the pistil on another flower of the same plant.

By deliberately crossing these pure-breeding lines, Mendel found that the 14 characteristics consisted of 7 pairs:

(1) A tall line, and a dwarf line;
(2) A line with green pods and one with yellow pods;
(3) A line with smooth pods and one with constricted pods;
(4) A line with round seeds and one with wrinkled seed coats;
(5) A line with gray-brown seed coats and one with white;
(6) A line with yellow cotyledons and one with green;
(7) A line with flowers where leaves arose and one with all its flowers at the end of the stem.

It made no difference in his crosses, such as between pure-line tall and pure-line dwarf, whether the tall plant contributed or received the pollen. In every case the peas from the cross would all grow to become a single kind of plant, in this case a tall one virtually indistinguishable from the tall pure-line ancestor. But Mendel did not stop his experiments with this first generation, which he called the "first filial" generation and represented with the symbol F_1. Carefully he self-pollinated each of the F_1 plants, collected their seeds and raised an F_2 ("second filial") generation. Among these, the dwarf form reappeared in about 25 percent of the plants; the rest (75 percent) were tall. But were these F_2 tall plants tall like the pure-line tall ancestor, or like the tall plants of the F_1? Mendel kept separate the peas from self-pollinating each of the plants in the F_2 generation, and raised an F_3 generation.

The outcome in the F_3 told him a great deal about the inheritance carried in the plants of the F_2 generation. Seeds from the self-pollinated dwarf plants in the F_2 gave only dwarf plants in the F_3. Dwarfness had not been contaminated by being concealed by tallness in the F_1 generation. The inheritable feature, which he called a "character," remained pure. In a hybrid, such as the F_1, dwarfness was simply concealed. He called it a "recessive character." Tallness, by contrast, was a "dominant character." But there was no way to predict in advance which of a matching pair of characters would be the dominant; only a test could give the answer.

Of the tall plants in the F_2 that Mendel self-pollinated, one third produced seeds that grew in every case to be tall plants. These must have been pure-line tall plants, concealing no character for dwarfness. The remaining two-thirds of the tall plants in the F_2 generation produced seeds that grew into both dwarf plants and tall plants. When all of these were added up, the proportion of dwarfs to tall proved to be about 1 in 4, or 1 to 3, just as in the F_2 generation. Hence the F_2 generation had actually contained pure-line dwarf, hybrids, and pure-line tall plants in the proportion 1 : 2 : 1 (or 25 percent : 50 percent : 25 percent). All seven pairs of true-breeding lines showed this same pattern of inheritance. In the numbered list above, the first-named line is the one that showed dominance.

In 1865, no one had any idea that chromosomes carried the inheritable features, or even how chromosomes participated in sexual reproduction, in cell division, in reduction division, or in alternation of generations. No one realized that each cell of a garden pea plant contained a double set of chromosomes: two of the number 1 chromosome, two of the number 2, and so on. No one knew that reduction division provided the spores with a single set of chromosomes apiece: one number 1 chromosome, one number 2, and so on. Equally unknown was the fact that the pairs of chromosomes in the zygote and the sporophyte plant included one "paternal chromosome" that came from the sperm cell and one "maternal chromosome" that came from the egg cell at the moment of fertilization. Reduction division separates paternal and maternal chromosomes, and parcels them out at random into the spores (pollen grains or ovules). The inheritance that has been separated in this way is perpetuated into the sperm cells and the egg cells in the flower, giving each one of these either a maternal or a paternal chromosome—but not both— in the single complete set of chromosomes within the gamete.

Despite the fact that these were mysteries in Mendel's day, he invented a set of symbols to represent his unit characters in pea plants and their mode of inheritance. Modified slightly toward modern usage, we can write capital letters for the dominant character and lower-case letters for the recessive, choosing the initial of the dominant for the letters to be used. Thus *TT* becomes the symbol for a pea plant of the pure-breeding tall line, *Tt* for a hybrid plant that grows tall, and *tt* for a pea plant of the pure-breeding dwarf line.

Whole plants are represented by double letters, their gametes by single letters. All gametes from a *TT* plant will be *T*, all from a *tt* plant will be *t*, but from the hybrid plant *Tt*, two kinds of gametes will form in equal proportions—*T*, and *t*. When a *TT* plant is self-pollinated or crossed with another *TT* plant, a gamete with *T* fuses with another gamete with *T* and reconstitutes the *TT* line of inheritance. Similarly with self-pollinating *tt* plants or crossing them with others of this constitution, a gamete with *t* fuses with another gamete with *t* and continues the *tt* line. But when hybrids of constitution *Tt* are self-pollinated or crossed with others of this type, a sperm with *T* may fuse with an egg with *T*, or a sperm with *T* may fuse with an egg with *t*, or a sperm with *t* may fuse with an egg with *T*, or a sperm with *t* may fuse with an egg with *t*. Each combination is equally probable. The outcome will be one *TT* for each two *Tt* for each one *tt*.

Today we know the cellular background and realize that two homologous chromosomes, perhaps the number 1 chromosomes,* in the hybrid plant bear at matching sites along their length the molecules that serve as genetic determiners (called

---

* By custom, chromosomes are given numbers, starting with number 1 for the longest, number 2 for the next shorter, and so on.

genes); on one chromosome of the pair, the gene is in the dominant condition shown by T, and on the matching chromosome, the gene is in the recessive condition shown by t. Eventually, in the pollen tubes from pollen produced by such a plant, there will be an equal probability that the sperm cells will carry a chromosome with the dominant gene T as that they will carry the gene in the recessive (t) condition. Similarly in the ovules produced on such a plant, the egg cell will have a single set of chromosomes and one of these will carry the gene in either the dominant condition (T) or the recessive (t). Each ovule with its single egg has an equal chance either way. Mendel's symbols, chosen because they matched the outcome of his tests, correspond perfectly with the chromosomes and the genes these carry.

Mendel proceeded to more ambitious tests, refining his pure lines until he had matching pairs that bred true for two characters at a time, or for three characters. A pure line of tall plants with round seeds, for example, when crossed with an equally pure line of dwarf plants with wrinkled seeds, gave an F_1 generation in which all plants were tall with round seeds. When self-pollinated to get an F_2 generation for study, the doubly hybrid plants provided seeds of which 25 percent were wrinkled and 75 percent were round. When the wrinkled seeds germinated and grew up, 25 percent of them produced dwarf plants and 75 percent tall plants. Similarly among the round seeds that Mendel planted: 25 percent grew to be dwarf plants and 75 percent to be tall. The familiar ratios remained intact.

When this experiment was continued for one more generation, to the F_3, keeping exact records of the source and fate of each seed, Mendel found that he had some new combinations: pure-line individuals for tallness and wrinkled seeds, and others for dwarfness and round seeds. These pairs of unit characters, when combined in the F_1 plants, had segregated out with complete freedom. Every one of the seven pairs of characters in Mendel's experiments showed this same independence.

Mendel applied his symbolic letters to this type of inheritance too. Revised slightly to follow modern notation, this would show the pure-line tall, round-seeded pea plants as *TTRR* and the pure-line dwarf, wrinkled-seeded plants as *ttrr*. The former would provide *TR* in their gametes and the latter *tr*, making the hybrids *TtRr*. The outcome of self-pollinating these F_1 plants could not be foreseen, but with evidence from the F_2 and F_3 generations, Mendel could conclude reliably that four kinds of inheritance had been passed from the F_1 generation, in equal proportions. They were *TR*, *Tr*, *tR*, and *tr*. Among the F_2, he found plants produced by combination of *TR* with *TR*, *Tr* with *Tr*, *tR* with *tR*, and *tr* with *tr*, all of which were pure-line types able to perpetuate their kinds when self-pollinated. All other combinations appeared too, and in the proportions that he could have predicted only if the characters were inherited independently.

Our modern explanation for his results is more satisfying, since it is based upon the segregation of chromosomes during the reduction divisions. The same rules hold when spores are being produced, whether they are to become pollen grains or ovules. As the seven homologous pairs of chromosomes of the garden pea plant undergo this special division, the separation of paternal chromosomes from maternal chromosomes may give

to one spore	*and to another spore*
a paternal #1 chromosome	a maternal #1 chromosome
a maternal #2 chromosome	a paternal #2 chromosome
a paternal #3 chromosome	a maternal #3 chromosome
a paternal #4 chromosome	a maternal #4 chromosome
a maternal #5 chromosome	a paternal #5 chromosome
a maternal #6 chromosome	a paternal #6 chromosome
a paternal #7 chromosome	a maternal #7 chromosome

Unless the paternal and maternal cells were identical in all but sex, the inheritance provided in these spores will certainly be different. A total of 128 different possible combinations of paternal and maternal chromosomes are equally likely. This number comes from the choice between two made simultaneously in seven different features (chromosomes), as $(2)^7$. With the genetic heritage shared among a larger number of chromosomes, the variation provided by reduction division is correspondingly increased. With its 21 different chromosomes, the cultivated wheat plant of the *vulgare* type produces $(2)^{21}$ combinations, which is 2,097,152 unlike. A person, with 23 homologous pairs of chromosomes, provides 8,388,608 different combinations, which is $(2)^{23}$.

By sheerest chance, the unit characters that Mendel used in his experiments were independent in their assortment when tested two or more at a time. Each of the seven pairs of matching genes, a dominant and a recessive, was carried by a separate chromosome among the seven different chromosomes in the set segregated out to a spore and replicated into the gamete. Mendel could not have found an eighth pair of unit characters without running into the phenomenon of linkage. Suppose, for example, that a character we can represent by *A* and *a* in the dominant and recessive forms were carried close to the genes for tallness and dwarfness on the same homologous pair of chromosomes. A pure-breeding line *TTAA* would produce spores *TA* and eventually contribute gametes with *TA*. Similarly a pure-breeding line *ttaa* would lead to gametes with *ta*. The zygote *TtAa* would develop into a plant showing both dominant characters. But this member of the F_1 generation could produce spores with only two kinds of genetic constitutions: *TA* and *ta*. A single chromosome would carry both in either the maternal or the paternal combination. In the F_2 there would be only plants showing both dominants (*TTAA* and *TtAa*) and those with neither dominant (*ttaa*) in the proportion of 3 : 1.

Linked genes were discovered first in the little fruitfly, which has only four pairs of homologous chromosomes. Irregularities in inheritance of linked genes led to techniques for mapping the location of genes along the length of the chromosomes, and to a realization that the genetic determiners have a fixed position and hence probably a molecular configuration.

THE GENETIC DETERMINERS

Until 1953, no one could imagine how any of the chemical substances found in chromosomes could operate as genes do. There had to be a molecule that could be replicated faithfully at every cell division for thousands of years. It had to be modifiable, from the dominant condition to the recessive or the converse, especially when subjected to X rays or other penetrating types of radiation. It had to control, directly or indirectly, the chemical activities within each cell, for these are the basis of maintenance, growth and reproduction—all following the rule that "like begets like."

Then a team of scientists who had been carrying on research in Britain and the United States proposed that the molecule with suitable properties was that of deoxyribonucleic acid, or DNA for short. Combining all of the information about it, these scientists concluded that this type of molecule could come in many lengths but always with the shape of a twisted ladder they called a "double helix." The lengthwise strands, between which crossbars stretched like rungs, could be composed of deoxyribose (a sugar with 5 carbon atoms) and inorganic phosphate. The rungs could be similarly simple, each composed of two nitrogen-containing bases, one a purine (either guanine or adenine) and the other a pyrimidine (either cytosine or thymine). The only combinations that would hold together and fit between the lengthwise strands would be guanine linked to cytosine, or adenine to thymine. Yet, as visualized from one side of the ladder, the rungs could have four different patterns: adenine-thymine, which could be represented by the letter A; thymine-adenine, by T; cytosine-guanine, by C; or guanine-cytosine, by G. These four letters could be thought of as a genetic code.

The code could be copied exactly at each ordinary cell division if the DNA molecule splits lengthwise from one end, separating consecutive rungs between the purine and pyrimidine of each. If the cell supplied new thymine to go with each exposed cytosine, and cytosine to go with each exposed guanine, and then linked these newly added units by a suitable lengthwise strand, it would have two complete molecules of DNA with exactly the same sequence of code letters in the crossbars. Precise replication of this kind would match the known stability of the genetic heritage through repeated cell divisions.

A change, called a mutation, could be as simple as the alteration of a single rung, perhaps by turning it end for end to transform A into T, or C into G. This might occur spontaneously at long intervals, or more frequently if the DNA molecule were bombarded by ionizing radiations (such as X rays) or subjected to particular kinds of poisons in the cell.

The code might be transcribed into a suitable single-stranded molecule and the coded information carried from the particular site in the specific chromosome to various centers in the cell where proteins were being synthesized. There the code might be read in terms of the sequence of amino acids to be incorporated into the protein molecule. The protein, in turn, serves as the facilitating agent (called an enzyme or organic catalyst) for a definite chemical reaction, which will not take place without the correct protein. Hence the coded pattern in the DNA—the molecule of the gene— in the chromosome could determine what chemical reactions were possible, and hence how a cell could maintain itself, grow and reproduce.

Subsequent experiments have shown that the genetic code is read three rungs at a time, which provides 64 combinations such as AAA, AAT, AAC, AAG, ATA, ATT, ATC, ATG, and so on. On this basis, a molecule of DNA of average size could encode the directions for making a protein with 500 amino acids in sequence, which is about the average size among proteins.

During the 1960's, the genetic code was deciphered completely. So was the sequence of amino acids in a few different kinds of proteins, mostly those of less than average size. Artificial genes were constructed and injected into living cells, which promptly followed the coded misguidance. They synthesized sequences of amino acids that confirmed the reality of this molecular control system, but that had no use in life. The next logical step will be harder: to synthesize a useful molecule of RNA or DNA and correct the deficiencies of a cell that is handicapped through its inheritance.

GENES AND VIRUSES

Microbiologists, who study infectious diseases of plants and animals, have discovered that the extremely small microbes known as viruses can reproduce themselves only inside suitable living cells. The virus particle consists of a sheath of protein around a long molecule or chain of molecules of either DNA or the messenger substance called RNA (ribonucleic acid). The RNA can transfer the coded instructions to the centers in a cell where proteins are being synthesized. In either case, the virus attaches itself to a susceptible cell by means of its protein cover, and injects the DNA or RNA. Inside the cell, these foreign molecules induce the synthesis of both protein sheath material and also more of the particular DNA or RNA. Automatically, the sheaths and DNA (or RNA) combine to form more virus particles. Generally the cell dies, breaks open, and releases the particles where they can continue their attack.

The virus particles can be cleaned of all extraneous matter, dried, and stored indefinitely like crystals of chemical compounds. In this condition, they need no energy. Yet their infective characteristics remain unimpaired. Scientists are still trying to learn whether a virus can properly be regarded as alive. The simplest of them, such as the $T2$ virus that attacks bacterial cells of the common sort found in the human digestive tract, seem to have a DNA molecule long enough to specify the synthesis of just two different compounds: the protein for the sheath, and another length of DNA. By contrast, the smallest bacterial unit that can absorb its own nourishment and carry on syntheses within its own membrane has enough genetic determiners to control about 40 different reactions. A colon bacillus, such as the $T2$ virus attacks, is larger and has the genes to match about 3,000 different syntheses. This is still a small number, whem compared to the genes in any cell of the human body, which could specify the enzymes for between 60,000 and 80,000 chemical reactions.

The genes of bacteria are receiving intense study, for several reasons. They are few enough—although apparently never less than 40—for the geneticist and molecular biologist to be hopeful about understanding their interaction in the near future. The life history of each cell is brief and, excluding the rare sexual interchange of genetic heritage, subject to repetitive asexual sequences in reproduction. The possibility of discovering a new way to control harmful bacteria is always open.

Among the recent discoveries is a realization that genes act in a chronological order, generally in relation to chemical changes that have already taken place in the cell. Some genes are now known to be "repressor genes," which prevent other genes from becoming active until the proteins they specify will have a role in the life of the individual. Probably in vascular plants, many genes are never turned on for the simple reason that the processes they once controlled are no longer needed; they relate to operations that were important during much earlier times, millions of years ago. They have not been dropped from the genetic heritage because the replication process keeps producing them in a form that causes no harm.

EXTRA CHROMOSOMES AND EXTRA VIGOR

During the past and right up to the present day, the behavior of chromosomes has occasionally failed to follow the normal pattern. In a leaf or some part of a flower that did not contribute directly to formation of reproductive cells, the error might be replicated at subsequent cell divisions and then lost when the leaf fell or the seeds were dispersed. But in the growth center of a stem or root, a daughter cell that received all of the chromosomes that ordinarily would be shared equally by two cells takes on a new genetic nature. Instead of containing a double set of chromosomes, it would have four sets. Since plant chromosomes generally occupy only a small portion of the total space in the cell, the extras may present no difficulties for a while. Yet if the cell with the quadruple set replicates them all each time it divides, and continues until it elaborates a whole stem with flowers, it leads to formation of gametes with a double set of chromosomes instead of a single set.

The fusion of a gamete with two sets of chromosomes and another with a single set induces no immediate disaster in most plants. The zygote with its triple set of chromosomes can undergo ordinary divisions, which replicate every chromosome present regardless of number and provide identical triple sets in each daughter cell of the sporophyte plant. The difficulty arises when reduction division begins in formation of spores. There is no easy way to divide three of each kind of chromosome into two daughter cells. Often the outcome is complete sterility for the plant.

But if a flower whose cells each contain a quadruple set of chromosomes forms its spores with double sets and these lead to gametes with double sets, and then self-pollination occurs, the zygote has four sets of chromosomes. It can grow into a normal plant and, when it comes to reduction division toward its own reproduction, can often produce spores with double sets of chromosomes. This genetic line may be fertile when crossed with other plants of the same species that possess the quadruple number of chromosomes.

These peculiarities might have been merely scientific curiosities if three observations had not been made. First, plants with double the normal number of chromosomes often grow larger, prove to be hardier, and show greater range in color and other features that man admires or can turn to use; in crop plants or horticultural specimens, these are mostly gains with definite commercial value. Secondly, a great many kinds of wild plants are found to have in a single genus a species or two with one chromosome number, several more species with twice this number, and perhaps a few with three times or even four times the lowest number of chromosomes; generally the ones with the most chromosomes are also the most widely distributed and aggressive species, with a clear advantage in their style of growth. And thirdly, with a one-percent solution of the drug colchicine obtained from the plant known as the autumn crocus, a horticulturalist can often induce doubling of the chromosome number in enough cells of immersed cuttings to be able to deliberately start new genetic lines.

A cell with a double set of chromosomes is said to be diploid; one with three sets is triploid; one with four sets is tetraploid, or simply grouped with any plant having more than three sets as being a "polyploid." Einkorn wheat is a diploid, whereas the more desirable emmer wheats are tetraploid, and *vulgare* wheats have six sets of chromosomes in each cell of the sporophyte plant. Fifty years ago, almost all of the garden iris plants were diploids; "modern" types developed by horticulturalists are mostly tetraploids.

Even crosses between species can sometimes be arranged by skillful use of colchicine. A few years ago, a breeder tried crossing ordinary cabbage, which has a diploid number of 20 chromosomes, with Chinese cabbage, which has a diploid number of 18. The experiment yielded a few seeds, which grew into a strangely different plant with 19 chromosomes in each cell. It was sterile. But the breeder put some cuttings of it in a colchicine solution, and obtained some branches with 38 chromosomes. The flowers they produced proved to be sterile too. But when this strange and vigorous plant with its 38 chromosomes was crossed with rutabaga (a turnip with a diploid number of 38 chromosomes), a new leafy vegetable grew from the seeds. It too had 38 chromosomes, but it was fertile and bred true. Now the only problem is one of marketing—finding people who are willing to try a new food, enjoy it, and make cultivating the "colbaga" worthwhile.

7

Plants in the Balance of Nature

For at least a billion years, plants have lived in the seas. More than 400 million years ago, some of them spread into fresh waters and began colonizing the land. They became adapted to the climatic conditions in arid and alpine regions only about 60 million years before modern times. Now it is hard to imagine the world without plants. They have taken an essential place in the balance of nature.

The green plants can be credited with freeing into the earth's atmosphere essentially all of the oxygen it contains, and with maintaining the concentration at about 21 percent despite all of the oxidative processes, such as respiration and combustion. In the process of photosynthesis, from which the oxygen is a waste byproduct, they capture energy from sunlight and store a surplus beyond their current needs. The surplus, in the form of the binding energy that holds together the atoms of organic compounds, not only allows green plants to survive during adverse climatic conditions (such as night, and drought, and winter) but also nourishes all other forms of life, either directly or indirectly. On land, moreover, the green plants retard the geological forces of erosion and have a major role in slowing the return of meltwater and rain toward the sea. This gives many kinds of life a chance to use the water and to survive where they could not otherwise.

The nongreen plants too influence the world profoundly. The decomposers among them are the principal agents of sanitation, simplifying the nonliving products of plants and animals—both dead bodies and wastes. They release carbon dioxide, water, and mineral nutrients where these can be re-used, and tend to balance the energy budget of the earth by freeing in the form of radiant heat the remainder left by green plants and animals from the solar energy captured through photosynthesis. With the help of some of the animals, the nongreen plants transform a static mixture of mineral particles into a dynamic soil. This action helps keep moisture where it is useful to living things of many kinds, and adds an extra habitat where both plants and animals can live or take shelter.

Generally we think of the parasitic plants—particularly those that cause disease—as undesirable members of the living community. So often they attack plants or animals that we cherish, shortening their lives. Only by suppressing our personal involvement with the diseased individuals can we find a true perspective. On a time scale measured in centuries or millennia, the parasites may be merely eliminating plants or animals that represent a surplus and that are not needed to ensure survival of the species into an indefinite future. Diseases have an important role in control of populations—preventing them from growing beyond their natural resources.

All nature continues in a state of unstable balance. If a mutation confers a slight improvement in the fitness of some species of plant for its environment, or a change in the environment favors this particular kind of vegetation, its increased success leads to an increase in population. But with more plants of the same kind in an area, opportunities improve for the disease agents and animals that attack the particular type of plant. The bacteria and fungi travel from infected plants to healthy ones more easily. The animals find more of a favorite food for themselves and their young. Consequently, although there are more plants present, their ability to stay healthy and whole enough to reproduce diminishes. Their surviving seedlings may actually be fewer than before the mutation occurred or the change in the environment favored the increase in numbers. Yet if the population decreases somewhat, the agents of disease and the animals that eat the particular plant find fewer of them. With a lessening of attack, the plants have greater success in reproduction and the population increases again.

Each species of living thing goes through these changes in numbers. In every new generation it encounters resistance in the environment, tending to keep its numbers low. In each new generation, those individuals with inherited features that meet the challenges of the environment are the ones that reproduce most effectively. They are best able to express their potential for increasing the size of the population. Scientists who study the interaction between living things call themselves ecologists. They refer to the balance of nature as a consequence of countless adjustments between the environmental resistance encountered by each species, and the biotic potential of the species—its readiness to reproduce.

Merely because a mutation gives no lasting superiority and greater size of population does not mean that it has no value to the species. Ordinarily the change in inherited features is continued. Still more changes may affect it. For example, many of the acacia trees in warm countries include in their inheritance the detail in growth that produces spines along the branches, often where the leaves arise. Supposedly, a great many more animals would eat the leaves and branches of the acacia tree if it did not have the spines. But some animals either avoid the spines, as caterpillars can, or they manage to eat spines and all, as giraffes and elephants do. Some of these trees have added another mutation: a space within each spine and a small hole connecting the cavity to the outside world. A few even have, within the cavity, some small glands that secrete a substance attractive to ants. Ants make use of these cavities as ready-made nurseries in which to lay eggs and tend their young, and often to store some food. If the tree is jostled, the ants rush out to defend their young and food, biting and stinging any animal, including caterpillars. By adding one inherited feature to another, the tree has attracted animals that will do it no harm and that will defend it. A great many features have obvious value to the plant in this and other ways. They are referred to as adaptations.

ADAPTATIONS RELATED TO NOURISHMENT

For a green plant to be well nourished, it must reach light and supplies of water and dissolved inorganic matter. Minute plants that drift in the sea have all the water they can use, and often enough dissolved mineral substances. But to stay in the light, they must remain near the surface. They need oil droplets, such as diatoms produce, or some other buoyant mechanism to keep them from sinking ever deeper into darkness. Many of the kelps and smaller seaweeds along the coasts possess gas bladders that raise their fronds to the light. These are adaptations related to nourishment.

Algae that lack both oil droplets and gas bladders can grow in the lighted levels of the sea by holding fast to rocks or producing a mass of spreading branches that remain imbedded in the sea floor. These adaptations must be started early in life and the grasping parts enlarged to keep the plant in place. While holding on where it has light, the alga also resists the force of waves and storms. These must not cast it from the sea into dry air, where it could get neither enough moisture nor the essential dissolved inorganic materials.

Whether in the sea near the shore or on land, most green plants with fronds or leaves spread these with one flat surface toward the light. They grow in ways that tend to keep one part from shading another as though making a mosaic pattern. This special type of growth and the sensitivity to shading that controls it are common adaptations toward getting energy that we often overlook.

In a forest, especially in a rainy region of the tropics, it is easy to appreciate the importance of thick, strong tree trunks in holding the leaves high above the ground toward the light. Less obvious is the role of the trunk in carrying water from the earth to the foliage, and elaborated organic foods from the leaves to the sturdy roots below ground. In the darkness of the soil the roots cannot make their own food, but they can absorb water and mineral nutrients for the whole tree, and keep it solidly upright despite the force of gravity and an occasional violent wind.

A surprising number of different kinds of plants show special abilities in clambering over rocks and vegetation too, or in climbing. We call them vines, and often notice how their stem tips reach out, perhaps gaining extra stiffness by several twining together, until they can catch on a tree limb or other support. English ivy climbs walls by extending from its stem along the zone of contact a long series of short, stiff, adventitious roots that penetrate minute cavities and hold tightly. Boston ivy has special branches ending in a number of small, circular, sticky pads with which it can cling to surfaces as smooth as glass or enamel paint. Sweet pea plants have their tendrils, which coil about stems or other supports and then undergo a special double twisting that tightens the plant in place. All of these are adaptations related to holding the plant where it can get light, and consequently relate to its nourishment.

In parts of the world where dry weather returns every year, or in deserts where drought is chronic and rain a rare event, plants generally have far more light than they can use. Yet they cannot nourish themselves through photosynthesis unless they can reach water far underground, or possess a hoard of moisture to call upon. A tremendous system of branching roots extending deep into the soil is the successful adaptation of the clover-like crop plant known both as alfalfa and lucerne. It serves the plant well in its native home, along the fringes of the deserts in North Africa. It helps alfalfa grow luxuriantly in the semiarid lands of north-central and western North America, to which it was introduced nearly a century ago as a food for domestic cattle.

The conspicuous adaptation of the cacti that are so varied in the American Southwest is their water-hoarding tissue in stems that sometimes resemble flat leaves. The story is often told that a thirsty person in the desert can cut off the top of a barrel cactus 2 feet tall and a foot in diameter, then hollow out a basin-shaped cavity and let the plant fill it with drinking water. Unfortunately, the cactus will do no such thing. The cut surface will simply dry off and harden, preventing further loss of moisture. And if the pulpy center of the cactus is scooped out as a material that might yield gallons of water if squeezed, the product is scarcely worth the squeezing. A cupful or two might be obtained, but it would be thick, almost a syrup, with very little flavor or with an unpleasant taste. The cactus would not live long if every thirsty animal that passed could raid its hoarded moisture and get a refreshing drink.

Cacti of American deserts

Yuccas and century plants hoard moisture in their short vertical stems, which are mostly underground, and in the thick sharp-pointed leaves that radiate out from the top of the stem in a tight rosette. These plants, like the cacti, store organic foods in these same places. Century plants got their name because the pioneering people who discovered them believed that these plants live one hundred years before flowering, and then die as the single crop of fruits begins to ripen. The century plant does die after flowering, but ordinarily it can accumulate enough nourishment in ten to twenty years to be able to produce quickly its tall upright stalk of flowers. In just a few weeks, this stalk grows to a height of 15 feet or more. In its flowers, the plant offers free nectar—a dilute solution of flavorful sugars—to any bird or fruit bat or insect that will come and distribute the pollen.

The last of the moisture and the food materials that the century plant collects and stores, using the special adaptations that fit it for this program under desert conditions, is

Yucca—a desert lily

transferred into its thousands of seeds. As in so many other seed plants, the adaptive features relating to nourishment serve ultimately to provide a reserve for a generation that has yet to develop. The embryo will use this store during its period of dormancy in the seed, and later while it resumes growth as a young seedling.

The nongreen plants have different requirements in life. Since they cannot gain their energy from light directly, they must either invade the cells of green plants or reach organic compounds they can digest and then use as food. The parasitic fungi and bacteria, and the few flowering plants (such as dodder) with parasitic habits and no chlorophyll, invade the other living things that serve them as involuntary hosts. The nonparasitic types of nongreen plants are all fungi and bacteria, collectively called saprophytes ("decay plants"), because they secrete digestive juices against the organic matter they reach, and then absorb simpler products of digestion. Whatever is left over as waste from the activities of one saprophyte becomes available to different saprophytes, until the wastes are substances from which no more energy can be obtained. Each parasite shows a whole galaxy of adaptations that match the characteristics of the host it attacks. Each saprophyte shows fewer specialties, except in the small array of digestive juices it can secrete to make its food absorbable.

ADAPTATIONS THAT ARE VALUABLE IN DEFENSE

When we think of a plant needing to defend itself, the hazards that come to mind first are likely to be animals that might eat its buds and leaves, suck the elaborated foods from its phloem cells in stem and root, or tunnel through its bark to reach the nourishment beneath. The bark is clearly advantageous in many ways: it shuts out all but a few kinds of small animals, and prevents damage to the delicate living cells inside when large animals rub against the tree to relieve an itch; it holds in moisture, and may serve for a while as thermal insulation against sudden changes in temperature, such as when fire sweeps through, over the forest floor.

The smaller hazards are often much more numerous: the bacteria, the fungus spores, and insects less than a quarter of an inch long. To meet these, the plant needs chemical adaptations that make it unattractive. Yet no matter what poisons it produces, some kind of insect seems able to eat it without being killed. Milkweed plants, for example, contain a poisonous resinoid as well as a distasteful, repellent "milk." Yet the milkweed caterpillar (the immature stage of the monarch butterfly) and the milkweed longhorn beetle (whose larvae bore for food in milkweed stems and roots) not only tolerate these substances but contain so much of the poisonous and distasteful materials from the milkweed that few birds will eat them. Fortunately for the green plants, the numbers of insects are kept low by bacterial diseases and parasitic fungi. This explains how so many milkweed plants go undamaged. The complex interrelations among living things ordinarily prevent outbreaks and serious destruction.

ADAPTATIONS RELATING TO DISPERSAL OF SPORES

Sometimes an adaptive feature seems extremely simple, such as producing spores as high up as possible on the plant, where the wind is more likely to carry these dust-sized particles to new locations. This is part of the secret of success of mushrooms and puffballs, earth-stars and morels, which grow as meshworks of pale threads in the soil of forests and fields. The threads reach organic compounds and digest them. Eventually the inconspicuous plant accumulates enough food reserves to send up a spore-producing structure. This too may be hidden at ground level for a few days. Then it grows into the open, attains its characteristic shape, and produces spores. The spores of a mushroom arise from minute knobs that project from the vertical surfaces of thin vanes (called gills) or slender tubes (called pores) which open underneath the spreading cap. The characteristic color of the spores can be discovered by making a "spore print." The cap of the mushroom is cut off and laid with its gills or pores downward atop a sheet of white paper. Over it is inverted a

Reproductive
parts of fungi

drinking glass that has been rinsed and drained (but not dried), to keep the humidity high for a day or so. The spores usually drop on the paper in obvious lines or small dots. If sprayed with plastic, the print will last.

The spores of a puffball or an earth-star dry to a brown powder inside the outer covering of the ball-shaped reproductive body, and are lifted out by wind as it passes any small hole or tear in the top. Morels shed their spores from slender sacs of microscopic size on the moist surface of the irregular cavities that give this kind of fungus a spongy appearance.

Often the vegetative parts of a field mushroom keep growing in the upper levels of the soil, using up their food in a central area and spreading out from there at a fairly uniform rate. After a rain they may be ready to send up reproductive parts. As the mushrooms appear in this way, they mark the perimeter of a "fairy ring." They disperse their spores and decay. But the vegetative threads keep growing. In a month or so, they may send up another ring of mushrooms—this time bigger in diameter, and showing the rate at which the fungus threads are exhausting the organic matter they can digest underground.

Green plants of the land produce their spores in season. Mosses raise their spore cases on thread-thin stalks, and release the spores through the top. The opening through which the wind can lift the spores is protected in wet weather by an

An earth-star fungus

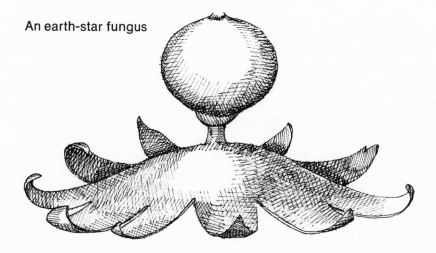

encircling series of thin triangular structures with their points toward the center. As soon as the humidity decreases, they curl back out of the way; until the last of the spores is gone, these points remain ready to uncurl and protect it from getting wet.

The "clubs" of clubmosses are clusters of spore cases on upright stalks that reach into whatever wind blows close to the ground where clubmosses grow. Horsetails bear their spores in clustered spore cases too, at the top of the stem. Ferns, whose fronds are true leaves, can best be identified by the location of their spore cases on the underside of fronds or on special leaves which have lost their flat blade portions and role in photosynthesis while becoming more efficient in getting spores airborne.

The "naked-seeded" plants (gymnosperms) rely upon the wind to disperse their pollen grains, each of which is a spore containing a developing male gametophyte. All gymnosperms are woody plants, usually growing as shrubs or trees. The cones or other organs from which they release their pollen are borne high on the plant, where the wind is strongest. Swirling in the air, the minute grains may be carried for many miles. Pollen from eastern white pine has been collected as it fell on the deck of ships crossing the Atlantic Ocean from Europe while the vessel was still 450 miles from the nearest pine tree in America.

Seed plants of any kind that use the wind to carry their pollen succeed best when they grow in large stands of just a few species. The larger the forest of white pine, or of mixed fir and spruce, the surer it is that each tree will catch from the wind the pollen it needs for reproduction. A grove of aspen trees, a marshful of cattails, a prairie on which a different grass uses the air route for pollen each week in summer, or a field of maize is similarly successful. Yet each of these plants wastes prodigious amounts of pollen in grains that never reach their targets. Near a pine forest each river and lake becomes coated with golden dust from the trees when they are dispersing their spores in the breeze.

In parts of the tropics and the temperate zones where flying animals of various kinds are numerous, seed plants with attractive flowers have a great advantage. The animals, whether insects or birds or bats, learn which pattern of showy parts and which scents correspond to a place where nectar or some other reward can be found. They seek out these floral patterns and distinctive odors by night or day and, in reaching the reward, brush both against the sticky tip of the pistils that are ready to receive pollen and also against the anthers of the stamens that have pollen ready to be transferred. Even if a bee takes some of the pollen as food—part of its reward for visiting the flower—the plant is likely to benefit. Small as the insect is, it still can remember the features that distinguish one kind of flower from another, and will use its eyes and sense of smell to seek out one after another of the same kind or of just a few kinds. In this way it distributes pollen far more reliably than wind can near the ground or where many kinds of plants grow side by side.

Flowers show many adaptive features that help attract particular types of animals, almost to the exclusion of others. White flowers with deep throats, such as those of nicotine and jimsonweed, generally open at night when moths will hover and uncoil their long tongues to reach the nectar. Red flowers would not be seen in darkness; they offer their nectar by day. Those that are deep-throated and pendant appeal most to the hummingbirds of America and the sunbirds of Africa, which have long slender beaks and even longer narrow tongues. The distinctive flowers that hang downward on fuchsia plants and the pendant orange flowers on certain columbines match well the hovering habits of hummingbirds. The aloes of Africa have mostly orange, tubular, pendant flowers and also bare branches close below, upon which sunbirds can perch while probing upward with their beaks.

Wild carrot, with all of its small flowers clustered at the same level, provides a platform on which flies and small beetles alight, then crawl about, unwittingly distributing pollen while relishing tiny drops of nectar from individual

flowers. The small flowers in the center of a daisy head cooperate in the same way in supplying a common surface over
which a bee can walk, after being attracted to the flower by
the ring of display petals around the flower head. The flowers
whose petals provide the display are often sterile, producing
no seed themselves, but signalling to the pollinating insects with a pattern they can see from far off.

ADAPTATIONS RELATING TO DISPERSAL OF RIPE SEEDS

The airlifting of the lightweight dry fruits of dandelion
and milkweed, birch and elm, maple and ash, costs these
plants nothing more than a tuft of hair or a thin flat expanded
part that catches the wind. Aspens far up the mountain slopes,
willows and cattails by the pond or river, show similar adaptations and get free transport for their fruits. The famous
tumbleweeds gain from the wind in a different way, as each
mature plant dies, curls into a ball-shaped mass, breaks away
from its drying root, and rolls along over the flat countryside,
peppering the soil with its minute seeds.

Many of the seedlings that spring up on soil bared after
a fire or the abandonments of fields by a farmer who has
moved elsewhere, arrive on soil that suits them entirely
through the vagaries of the wind. Others are airlifted too,
but in the digestive tracts of birds which have swallowed a
whole fruit or pulpy covering around a seed, digested the
soft parts, and discarded the indigestible seeds in their
droppings. The American mountain ash tree, like the Eurasian
rowan, travel as seeds to distant localities in this way. So do
brambles and briars of the rose family, and the many kinds
of junipers. Junipers (including the one called red cedar,
which attracts cedar waxwings and other birds) seem to be
exceptions to the rule that conifers and other gymnosperms
have naked seeds. Actually the juniper "berry" is a thick,
pulpy seed coat, which offers nourishment to birds. Yews
attract animals which eat the fleshy cup-shaped mass of pulp
that almost surrounds each seed; this pulp, which is often
bright red and sweet-flavored when the seed is ripe, is an

Fruits that reward animals
as they disperse seeds

outgrowth from the end of the stalk that supported the seed, and hence not a fruit at all. Similarly, a strawberry is not a fruit in the ordinary sense, for the fleshy part is again the enlarged, flavorful end of the stalk on which the flower expanded. Embedded in its surface are tiny, indigestible fruits, each one containing a minute seed.

Botanists have drawn up a complex classification of fruits. But as adaptations that promote the dispersal of the seeds, fruits come in fewer categories. Some, such as the grains from grasses, are edible as soon as they are ripe and dry. But they also appeal to the hoarding instincts of small animals, from agricultural ants to mice and chipmunks, which store them underground. Skunks dig into the ant nests, scattering the grain. Badgers and other carnivores do the same with mice. Quite often the grain gets covered with loose earth, which hides it from birds but lets rain reach it, causing it to germinate and grow far from the grass plants where the hoarding animals collected their supply.

Cherries and peaches, like many other fleshy fruits with armor around their seeds, tempt animals to carry them off for some distance from the tree on which they grew, and then discard the armored seed. Left on the ground, the armor softens through the activities of decomposers. By then moisture may have entered and stimulated the embryo to resume growth, becoming a seedling. Even without the sweet flesh over the armor, a walnut or a hickory nut may be carried by a squirrel and carefully buried. Unless the squirrel returns to eat the seed after the shell has softened, the embryo is likely to germinate, adding another tree of its kind if the living conditions are suitable. Probably most oak trees are planted in a similar fashion by squirrels. In this case, the shell over the seed is much thinner, but the seed itself contains a bitter substance until it has been soaked for a while, such as after a rain that penetrates the soil where the squirrel has buried the seed. American Indians used to collect acorns and soak them in water to get out the bitter substance, then dry the seeds and grind them into an edible meal.

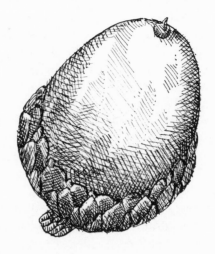

An acorn worth burying where it might grow to an oak

Almost everyone who has walked through an overgrown field in late summer, particularly along a narrow path with weeds along both sides, picks up an assortment of dry fruits that have hooks of various kinds. They catch on clothing, and also on the fur of wild animals. Generally known as burs, they include the individual fruits of the bur marigold (often known as "devil's pitchforks" because they have two or three barbed projections), whole dry flower heads of burdock, and fragments of the seed pods of tick-trefoil or "beggar's-ticks"—flat green sticky packets that project in chains of three or more from the tall herbaceous plant. These burs will eventually drop off, scattering the seeds at a considerable distance from the parent plant and often beside a path again, where the sequence can easily be repeated one generation after another.

An animal that steps accidentally on a sandbur generally reacts far more promptly. These fruits of a creeping grass that is common on sandy soil have needle-sharp spikes projecting from their ripe fruits. The spikes penetrate even tough skin and cause such immediate pain that the animal is almost sure to jump, and then to try in every way to free itself from the sandbur. If it tries to use its teeth to grip the spiny fruit, it may only transfer the sandbur to its lips. Minutes of acute discomfort may pass before the sandbur is dropped free. Generally this places it close to a game trail where another plant of the same kind can grow and again make use of animals to disperse its seeds.

If the adaptations of plants were rated according to how nearly worldwide they had induced a member of the Animal Kingdom to carry them, the top score would be a tie between various weeds and certain cultivated plants that man has introduced almost everywhere he has gone on continents and islands. Weed seeds have traveled as impurities in grain, as burs in wool shipped from one country to another, as trash in crates of machinery, and even in the gravel ballast scooped up and carried for no better purpose than to make unloaded ships ride more smoothly across the oceans.

SOCIAL ADAPTATIONS

Recently, someone tried to imagine how a visitor from elsewhere in the universe would interpret the activities of farmers cultivating crop plants. Quite easily the visitor might conclude that the plants are the masters, and men the oppressed slaves. Without commotion, the crops stay in one place and grow luxuriantly. Men rush to and fro, preparing the fields for new generations of the plants, carefully placing the seeds in the best locations, bringing mineral nutrients (fertilizers) and protective sprays of various kinds, gently harvesting the fruits, and storing them under ideal conditions or shipping them abroad to warehouses in which more men would work, tending the products of the plants.

Without human help, most of the crop plants could not survive under natural conditions. Native vegetation and weeds would crowd them out. But equally, human civilization could not maintain itself without food plants raised efficiently by modern agricultural methods. Ever since man domesticated certain grasses for their grains and other plant crops for food and fiber, these forms of vegetation have allowed expansion of human culture and human populations. The plants are culture-generators ("cultigens"), partners of the people who do the work of cultivation or benefit from the products. Neither side of the partnership can thrive without the other.

Plants have entered many partnerships. Single-celled algae cooperate with fungus plants in creating lichens, some of which tolerate climatic conditions of extreme severity. The same and other single-celled algae live in close association with somewhat larger single-celled animals (protozoans), with sponges, with coral animals and other coelenterates, free-living flatworms, and some exceptional mollusks such as the giant clams of coral reefs in the tropical Pacific Ocean. Both bacteria and certain fungi that grow separately in the soil also take up positions in the nodules on the roots of various flowering plants. In these nodules they show outstanding efficiency in converting gaseous nitrogen into nitrates, often in such profligate quantities that an excess spreads out in the soil and benefits adjacent plants. Still other fungi in the soil seem to specialize in enveloping the roots of coniferous trees, and of many heaths and orchids, in each instance serving in place of root hairs and aiding in the nourishment of the conspicuous partner. A few years ago in Puerto Rico, the value of these fungi was demonstrated in a pine plantation, where the introduced trees remained mere dwarfs. A teaspoonful of soil from a New England pine forest was sprinkled under the stunted pines in Puerto Rico. In the following year those particular trees grew 9 feet taller and kept on rising. The fungi, meanwhile, spread to surround the roots of other pines and aided their growth in the same way.

FOOD WEBS

When the interrelationships among living things were first investigated, the obvious features seemed simple enough to

arrange in a line called a food chain. Charles Darwin pointed
to one of these in his famous account of the way in which
house cats improve the vigor of clover fields. He noticed that
in red clover heads, the flowers secrete their nectar too deeply
for a honeybee to reach. The bigger bumblebees, with their
longer mouthparts, are the visitors that pollinate this clover.
The more bumblebees a red clover field attracts, he reasoned,
the more seeds it will produce, and the denser the clover
will grow.

But bumblebees build their honeypots upon the ground,
and tend their developing young there where field mice can
easily attack. Hence, the more field mice a clover field has
running around, the fewer will be the bumblebees that mature,
the fewer will be the clover seeds that mature, and the poorer
the clover will grow. Darwin ignored the hawks and other
predators that pounce on mice, and emphasized instead the
house cats that excel at catching mice. The more house cats
a farming region had, the fewer mice would be left to attack
nests of bumblebees, the more bumblebees would mature, the
more clover would be pollinated, and the better each clover
crop would be. Clover nectar to bumblebee young to field
mice to house cats is a food chain.

Today this food chain, like all others, is seen to have many
side connections which make it a food web. The welfare of
the clover is largely dependent upon the nitrogen-fixing bacteria in its root nodules, and these bacteria may suffer from
virus diseases. The roots and stems of the clover attract small
beetles with boring larvae. The caterpillars of at least two
kinds of butterflies come to feed on the clover leaves. A tiny
moth lays eggs on young clover leaves and its caterpillars
tunnel within the green tissue of the leaf. A fly produces
maggots that get their nourishment from developing seeds of
clover, killing the embryo plants. A parasitic bee, which re-
sembles a bumblebee in size, coloration and behavior, lays her
eggs in bumblebee nests, letting bumblebees feed her young—
which they do, even if their own become malnourished from
having to share the limited supply of food. All of these insects

have diseases and animal parasites of their own, and are fair prey for insectivorous birds. The field mice are attacked by agents of disease, by parasites such as fleas on the outside and tapeworms internally, by birds and beasts of prey native to the countryside as well as by house cats. These same predators and others destroy birds' eggs and nestlings, including those involved in the welfare of clover in one way or another. The predators have their diseases and parasites too—and all of the parasites have parasites! With so many branches in the food web, the number of house cats affects the clover crop chiefly where the native hawks, owls, foxes and weasels are few and the domestic animals substitute as predators.

Wild plants as well as cultivated ones vary in abundance according to the degree to which agents of disease and animals attack them, and also in relation to the weather during the growing season. So long as the food web is complex, the fluctuations in the abundance of any one particular kind are generally modest because so many alternatives are present. A slight decrease in the abundance of clover is quickly followed by a reduction in the number of insects that attack this plant. Some of them may be able to transfer their attention to other kinds of vegetation. Certainly the insectivorous birds that would ordinarily eat insect pests of clover will seek substitutes elsewhere. Nor are bumblebees dependent upon clover for their nectar supply. The whole system provides flexibility so long as many different species are interacting.

Often the balance of nature is severely distorted through man's use of land, particularly if the environment is deliberately simplified. A clover field or a pine forest is intended to produce only one kind of crop. Known as monoculture, it is an attempt to gain for mankind the maximum harvest before disaster strikes. By completely biasing the photosynthetic productivity of an area into materials useful in human culture, this gamble may succeed if all of the interactions between the crop plant and other living things—and the unpredictable weather—are favorable. If not, the area will produce nothing man can use. In any case, its production of organic matter will be distinctly less than if the same amount of sunlight and inorganic nutrients had been shared by a mixture of native vegetation.

Any single crop tends to deplete the soil. It removes particular nutrients and also nourishes only a select group of minute animals and those decomposers that can use fallen parts (such as petals and the lower leaves) and whatever roots die before and after the useful portions of the plant are harvested. All other living things in the soil soon become malnourished. Their continued activity is essential to keep the soil a suitable environment for roots. Farmers in many countries learned about a century ago to raise a different crop of cereals or vegetables or fiber plants in successive years, not repeating this rotational program oftener than every third or fourth year. At first this method gained approval merely because it improved the yield. Now farmers generally know why the change is needed, although often they are reluctant to include in each cycle a year "letting the soil rest" by allowing whatever plants come to colonize add variety to the field. The "fallow year" is a contribution, deliberate but beneficial over the decades and centuries, toward a natural balance in life, upon which all productivity depends.

8
Plants of the Past

A scientist who specializes on learning about plants in the recent and remote past is a paleobotanist. He has to be a skilled detective too because most of his evidence consists of fragments. Some of them are more than 600 million years old. Others dating from the last tenth of this immensity of time consist of pollen grains that fell into the cold dark waters of peat bogs, where tannins and other substances from dead peat moss stain the water and inhibit decomposition. Still others were preserved when the sticky gum of ancient pine trees flowed over them and turned to amber.

The first tasks of paleobotanists are to find and identify the remains of plants from long ago. Second, in many cases, is the challenge of establishing the date at which the plants died and were preserved. Particularly in the earlier periods of the fossil record, the plants were mostly small and soft— unsuited to preservation. Later, when vascular plants evolved and woody growth became common, pieces of root and stem were petrified by processes that replaced the watery proto-

plasm in the dead cells with crystals of lime or silica. Often
the cellulose and lignin of the cell walls remains in place,
and cellular details can still be examined in sections of the
fossil wood. In other instances, leaves made an imprint on soft
mud, and this pattern was preserved even if the tissues of
the leaves disappeared in the intervening millions of years.

Different methods, most of them invented during the last
two decades, are needed to establish the dates of fossils from
various periods in the past. Those from the most recent 30,000
years can often be learned by comparing the proportions of
ordinary carbon (carbon-12, symbol ^{12}C) and radioactive
carbon (carbon-14, symbol ^{14}C). While a green plant is alive,
or a nongreen plant is living on organic compounds from living
things or those quite recently dead, it incorporates into its
own organic compounds the carbon from atmospheric carbon
dioxide (symbol CO_2). In the atmosphere, the carbon dioxide
shows a relatively fixed proportion of the two forms of
carbon,* just a fraction of one percent being $^{14}CO_2$ and all the
rest the ordinary $^{12}CO_2$. So long as a green plant lives, it maintains the same proportion of ^{14}C to ^{12}C in all of the organic
compounds of its body. Nongreen plants and animals that get
their nourishment from green plants directly or indirectly
maintain this same proportion during their lifetimes. But
when a plant or animal dies, it no longer maintains an equilibrium with the two forms of carbon in the atmospheric
gases. Gradually the ^{14}C decays at a rate that is independent
of any feature in the environment. Delicate measurements
reveal that the rate of decay reduces the amount of ^{14}C remaining to a half in 5,770 years, which is known for this
reason as the "half-life" of the material. In another 5,770 years
(hence 11,540 years after the plant died), the ^{14}C is down to
a quarter; in 17,310 years to an eighth; in 23,080 years to a
sixteenth; and in 29,850 years to a thirty-second. Beyond this

* The stability represents an equilibrium between formation of ^{14}C
from ordinary nitrogen (nitrogen-14, symbol ^{14}N) in the upper atmosphere where cosmic rays are absorbed, and disappearance of ^{14}C by
the normal process of radioactive decay.

age, the remaining ^{14}C is so small that its radioactive emission (which is the feature measured) is scarcely more than comes as "background radiation" from recent materials in the laboratory. Five half-lifes of radioactive carbon-14 is the limit of the usefulness of this method for dating fossils that contain carbon.

A whole series of other chemical elements with radioactive isotopes and longer half-lifes are used in measuring the ages of specimens from longer ago.

2,000—2,000,000 years	"fission-track method," from the decay of uranium-238
10,000—200,000 years	"thorium-230/uranium-238 method," from deficiency of thorium-230
400,000—3,000,000 years	"potassium-40/argon-40 method," from increase in argon-40 due to decay of potassium-40
5 to 3,000 million years	"strontium-87/rubidium-87 method" from increase in strontium-87 due to decay of rubidium-87

Fortunately, the paleobotanist seldom has to rely upon a measurement made from a single fossil, because the same sedimentary rock or other fossil-bearing material ordinarily contains the remains of many other living things, both plant and animal. Supposedly the same date applies to all of them.

In performing his detective work, the paleobotanist relies also upon his excellent knowledge of modern plants, and on as much information as he can get about present-day biochemical similarities and differences, chromosome numbers and form, geographic distribution, and ecological relationships. Some of the earliest fossil remains of fungi, for example, are little thimble-shaped masses of threads in a tangle around the root tips of early trees. These would be hard to identify if many coniferous trees in modern times did not have fungi associated similarly with their roots.

Of course, erosion has destroyed a large proportion of the sedimentary rock and other media in which fossils were preserved. Geologists have found details of the fossil record extremely helpful in matching up strata with the same approximate age on different continents. They have reconstructed, too, some measures of the maximum thickness remaining in each layer of the same age, and used estimates for the rate of deposition to calculate the time required for formation of the maximum thickness. The whole history takes on a consecutive form, with only minor differences according to gross geography. It is usually represented in the form of a table showing the oldest periods (like the earliest rocks) at the bottom, and progressively younger ones above, up to modern times.

ERA	PERIOD (*duration shown in parentheses, as millions of years*)	BEGAN BEFORE PRESENT (*millions of years*)
Cenozoic	Quaternary, including Recent and Pleistocene (2)	2 million
	Tertiary, including Pliocene, Miocene, Oligocene, Eocene and Paleocene (61)	63 million
Mesozoic	Cretaceous (72)	135 million
	Jurassic (46)	181 million
	Triassic (39)	230 million
Paleozoic	Permian (40)	280 million
	Carboniferous (65)	345 million
	Devonian (60)	405 million
	Silurian (20)	425 million
	Ordovician (75)	500 million
	Cambrian (100?)	600 million?

Proterozoic (790?) ⎫   1,390 million?
                      ⎬ now often grouped as Pre-Cambrian times
Archeozoic (800?) ⎭   2,190 million?

Age of the planet Earth estimated to be about 4,500 million to 6,000 million

Age of our Universe (including stars in the Milky Way) 5,000 to 10,000 million

PLANTS OF PRE-CAMBRIAN TIMES

In Australia, Europe and North America, geologists have located rock outcroppings that consist entirely of sediments deposited nearly a billion years ago in seas and fresh waters. Those in the Medicine Bow Mountains of Wyoming have a total thickness of at least 24,000 feet. They include mineral matter piled up during three separate periods of glaciation, and also layers each more than 450 feet thick with the characteristics of particles collected at the bottom of glacial lakes.

No indications of life have yet been found in the lower 15,000 feet of this immense rock mass. But in the upper 9,000 feet the nature of the sediments changes from being the remains of ancient gravels, sands and muds. Instead, these upper strata consist of marble in successive levels, separated by material that once was clay. So far as is known, marble and other limestones are rarely produced except by living things, which absorb the lime from sea water and then deposit it as corals and coralline algae do today.

The marble in the Pre-Cambrian strata of Wyoming shows many columnar masses 8 feet in diameter and 10 feet or more in height. Each mass probably is the work of a patch of seaweed. In successive levels of the marble, the size and shape of these fossilized remains changes significantly. Yet in each, the details suggest to paleobotanists that the algae were blue-greens, or possibly lime-secreting reds. No remains or traces of animals have been found in these strata, nor any sign of plankton plants. But some microscopic rod-shaped bodies suggest the presence of bacteria. Almost certainly there were planktonic kinds of life as well.

Geologists who have examined these upper Pre-Cambrian rocks with special interest have commented on the purity of the sand layers, and the absence of deposits from rushing rivers, such as sandstones containing rock chips and mud balls. They question whether deposits can have accumulated in so undisturbed a way if the land surfaces of the continent had been bare. Lacking fossilized remains of land life of any kind, the paleobotanist can only suggest that at this early date, algae and fungi may already have been in partnership in the form of shrubby little lichens similar to modern reindeer moss. Such a covering over the land would have broken the force of rain and retarded drainage, perhaps enough to reduce erosion. It is equally possible that the continents had no mountains near the areas where the sediments accumulated and were transformed into the rocks that have been found. Slow, meandering rivers that flowed across a broad coastal plain would not have upset the deposition of particles from the quiet waters of shallow seas.

PALEOZOIC PLANTS

Although both plants and animals probably lived in the marine environment for 1,500 million years before the beginning of the Cambrian period, few of them possessed shells or skeletons that might resist the forces of time and be recognizable from fossilized remains. Except for the calcareous algae, most of them may also have been small and easily destroyed. Larger animals seem to have appeared early in the Cambrian. Some of them encased their bodies in coverings of lime, or of organic skeletal materials such as the insects, crustaceans and other arthropods produce today. Yet conditions for fossilization may have improved too, for soft fluffy muds have consolidated into rock bearing imprints of medusae (jellyfishes) and worms of various kinds.

Amid fossils of sponges and spongelike animals, of corals and other creatures with nettling cells, of mollusks and echinoderms and lamp shells (brachiopods) and arthropods (particularly the trilobites), the paleobotanist looks in vain for evidence of vegetation other than calcareous algae. He feels confident that the blue-green algae and the bacteria were abundant, and that plant life must have diversified considerably. Otherwise how could so many kinds of animals nourish themselves, every one of them in shallow marine environments along the coasts of the continents or in still shallower seas that flooded much of North America, Central and South America, Siberia, the Indian peninsula, central Africa and

Australia before the Cambrian period came to a close. At times the continents must have been represented merely by clusters of low islands while sediments in the shallows were preserving evidence of Cambrian life in places that more recently were elevated into air again. Probably rocks from this same period will eventually be found where now the ice is so thick over Antarctica, for boulders containing the fossilized remains of Cambrian sponges have been dredged from the ocean floor just south of the Ross Sea.

Changes in the kinds of animals that left a fossil record have led to identification of the Ordovician period as a distinctly different time. Among the marine algae are the first that seem clearly to be members of the phylum Chlorophyta— green algae with chloroplastids of bizarre forms and with sexual (as well as asexual) methods of reproduction. They show a branching style of growth that would have been well suited to life in clear coastal waters. In addition, the lime-secreting algae remained numerous and widespread, forming great underwater meadows where animals lurked. Among these were jawless armored fishes, as the earliest known members of the phylum Chordata and of its major surviving subdivision, the vertebrates. But the fossil record still shows no trace of life on land, or of plants more complex than thallophytes. This does not prove that none existed, although conditions for existence in air must have been hazardous during much of the Ordovician period. Debris from volcanic action accumulated over large areas of the continents as the earth rumbled and raised up new mountains where flat lands and shallow seas had been previously.

Mountain building continued during the succeeding period, the Silurian. In northern Norway, southeastern Alaska and British Columbia, the peaks towered high enough for valley glaciers to form and transport rock fragments into great terminal moraines. Yet these mountains intercepted the moist winds so effectively that on the lee side the lowlands became deserts, with immense sand dunes and thick deposits of salt where shallow seas dried up completely. Along the coasts, however, the water must have been warm. Coralline algae and coral animals produced vast reefs. Among the accumulations of limestone and dolomite (limy rocks containing magnesium) are many strata that recently have been quarried, or mined carefully for the deposits of gold and tin they include. In the United States, fully a tenth of all the iron ore known and a fifth of the salt deposits are of the Silurian age. Seemingly the climate varied little from north to south. Perhaps these conditions favored the emigration of plants and animals from the seas into estuaries and fresh water. In sediments from these habitats that accumulated late in the period are the remains of the earliest known scorpionlike animals and millipedes. By becoming adapted to life where the salinity was low and variable, they were gaining the features that would let their descendants later colonize the land. Meanwhile, in the coastal seas, brown algae and red algae left the first clear indications of their presence.

Among the distinctive ways of life that have developed among the members of the Plant Kingdom in producing separate species, fully 95 percent now are shown by land plants. If for no other reason, the paleobotanist looks with special interest at the fossils from Devonian times since they include the earliest definitely terrestrial vegetation. Presumably all of the phyla of aquatic thallophytes were well established before the beginning of the Devonian, and have continued through the immensity of time to the present. But the pace of their evolution in the marine and freshwater environments did not match that of land plants once these developed ways to cope with desiccation by dry air and irradiation by sunlight of far greater energy than reaches aquatic vegetation.

The continued mountain building during the Devonian increased the number and the velocity of rivers, the erosive damage they inflicted on the land, and the deposition of the sediments they carried. Apparently this geologic activity also caused a lowering of many areas on each continent, letting sea water flow into an ever-changing system of shallows.

Through these the water currents moved, distributing heat from the tropics toward the poles and keeping the climate fairly uniform at most latitudes. Whether the earliest land plants got their initial hold along the muddy shores of brackish lagoons or fresh waters may never be learned. Their remains show them to have been leafless, rootless, branching stems with wood as part of their firm vascular tissue. Some of these plants were preserved and discovered in the Gaspé region of eastern Canada, others in southeastern Australia, and still others in eastern Scotland.

Since the Devonian period lasted about 60 million years, which is almost as long as between the time of final extinction of the great dinosaurs and the present, it afforded plenty of opportunity for the new land plants to diversify. At first, the only known terrestrial vegetation was the little shrubby *Psilophyton* discovered in 1859 by Sir William Dawson in the Gaspé. It was followed by other members of this subphylum of vascular plants (the Psilopsida), all in an order (Psilophytales) that became extinct within 30 million years—but not before a number of newer types of land plants evolved from these early ancestors. One type, the closest with living members, formed another order (Psilotales) with two surviving genera (*Tmesipteris* and *Psilotum*) and three species. Other types included the ancestral forms of clubmosses (subphylum Lycopsida), of horsetails (subphylum Sphenopsida), and of ferns (subphylum Pteropsida, class Filicineae). All of these were established as woody shrubs and trees before the end of the Devonian.

Paleobotanists are still trying to fit into this pattern some fossilized fragments of wood from the upper Devonian strata. Without matching foliage or reproductive parts they cannot tell whether or not these samples prove the existence 350 million years ago of trees already committed through their adaptive features to becoming gymnosperms of types found fossilized in the later, lower strata of the following Carboniferous period.

Just as the Devonian is widely known as the "Age of Fishes," so the Carboniferous is often called the "Coal Age" or the "Age of Amphibians." These popular names suggest only a small part of the momentous changes that were in progress. The first fishes with jaws did evolve in early Devonian times, apparently in fresh water. Some of them spread to the oceans and diversified there to become the most conspicuous feature of the fauna that became preserved as fossils. Back in fresh water, however, some of the fishes that remained became shaped by natural selection to possess lungs and lobelike fins. These strange animals began crawling out on shore, as the ancestors of the first amphibians. At about the same time, the earliest insects so far discovered made an appearance, and so did the first spiders—relying for food supposedly on the insects, all of which were wingless. These additions to the variety of life, like the elusive ancestors of the gymnosperm trees, provided a foundation for major events during Carboniferous times.

Geologists are often sorely tempted to divide the Carboniferous period into two because, both in the New World and the Old, the earlier half of the period produced almost exclusively sedimentary deposits and enclosed fossils from marine environments, whereas the later half was dominated by materials that accumulated in freshwater swamps on the continents. But the transition between the two does not coincide well. Eurasian geologists and specialists on the fossil record speak of the Lower Carboniferous and the Upper Carboniferous, whereas those in North America refer to the Mississippian and Pennsylvanian. In both, the deposition of organic matter that became transformed to coal and petroleum occurred in the second half of the period. It seems to have been due to an almost cyclic rise and fall of the land. While slightly below sea level, salt water flooded in and killed off the land plants to the margins of higher ground. Sand and mud built up layers on the bottom, later transforming it into sandstone and slate. When the land was elevated, dense swamp forests began to grow. They accumulated organic matter at a rapid pace, only to have these carbon-containing compounds buried at the next incursion of salt water with fresh sediments. With time the carbon compounds released their hydrogen and oxygen to become almost pure carbon or hydrocarbons, often with residual sulfur. These strata with coal are known in Eurasia as the "coal measures," while those in eastern North America are simply the coal seams that are mined from Pennsylvania down the Appalachian mountain chain.

The swamp forests consisted of plants belonging to orders that are mostly now extinct, although they left descendants that are classified in separate orders. The principal trees were giant clubmosses, giant horsetails, the coenopterid ferns, and two very different types of gymnosperms: the seed ferns (Cycadofilicales), whose foliage was fernlike, and the cordaites (Cordaitales) which bore long grasslike leaves or broad ones as much as three feet long on a branching trunk suggesting that of a modern pine. Many of these forest denizens attained a height of 100 feet or more, and showed annual rings of growth comparable to those now seen in conifers and angiosperm trees of the temperate zones.

Ancient trees of the late Paleozoic era

Before the end of the Carboniferous period, ferns of the modern order Filicales and true conifers (order Coniferales) appear among the fossilized remains. So do the earliest bryophytes, as low-growing liverworts, perhaps descended separately and during this period from ancestors among the green algae. Over the liverworts and between the bases of the trees in the swamp forests, amphibians of many sizes crawled about. Much of their food, which let them exist and diversify, must have been insects. These now included members of many orders that develop directly from immature to adult, as cockroaches and sucking bugs do. Present also were the largest dragonflies the world has ever known, a few of them attaining a wingspan of 27 inches. Presumably they were hawking after plant lice (aphids) and similar small flying insects, and becoming increasingly adapted in dexterous flight to follow any prey that dodged.

While these developments in North America and Eurasia were in progress, apparently sustained by a warm or temperate climate, the southern ends of Africa, South America, Australia and all of New Zealand were suffering from cold. The sedimentary deposits that correspond in time show in these areas large quantities of rock debris from huge glaciers. For the climate to be so different north and south of the Equator becomes more understandable if, until after the Paleozoic era, the southern Continents were farther from the northern ones than they now are. A great deal of evidence has been discovered within the last two decades that can be interpreted as showing that the Atlantic Ocean had not yet formed. It is thought that North America was joined broadly to Eurasia, minus India, in one huge northern land mass called Laurasia. South America fitted tightly against Africa, and this combination to Antarctica, Australia, and India as a southern land mass known as Gondwanaland. Until the spreading of the sea floor began, separating the continents of the Western Hemisphere from those of the Eastern, a vast expanse of ocean (the Tethys Sea) connected waters around the Malay Peninsula northward where India is today, then

west to join with the Mediterranean Sea. South of this arm of
the ocean, which ended blindly at the present site of the
Straits of Gibraltar, were the continents-to-be that still consti-
tuted Gondwanaland.

On these southern continental areas during the succeeding
Permian period, despite cold weather and volcanic activity
as well as a general elevation of the surface that kept to a
minimum any intrusions of shallow seas, forests flourished in
a fashion almost equal to that of the swamp trees in Carboniferous times. They left deposits of coal containing fine imprints of the tongue-shaped leaves of a seed fern (*Glossopteris*). Even on Antarctica, coal seams and *Glossopteris*
fossils have been found in considerable abundance. Accom-
panying the "*Glossopteris* flora" were animals of many kinds,
including some large amphibians. Somehow they managed to
survive on Antarctica after their relatives on other parts of
old Gondwanaland became extinct. Both the plants and the
amphibians were still there to be fossilized during the first
period of the Mesozoic era; they were discovered a few years
ago.

On the northern continental mass of Laurasia during the
Permian period, the land emerged from the sea, thrust up
fresh mountain chains or elevated old ones (such as the
Appalachians and the Urals), created deserts, and provided
harsher weather than had occurred for hundreds of millions
of years. Actually, the conditions may have been no more
challenging than at present. Yet for plants adapted to tropical
and subtropical climates, to plentiful moisture, it was a time
of real crisis. Gymnosperms and members of the modern order
of ferns (Filicales) completely replaced the tree-sized clubmosses and horsetails, and the coenopterid ferns. Yet seed
ferns, including *Glossopteris*, rapidly colonized northward as
far as Greenland.

True conifers, which had made a modest appearance in the
Upper Carboniferous period, were well represented in the
Permian. Two new groups of gymnosperms arose: the ginkgoes
or maidenhair trees (order Ginkgoales), of which one species

survives today as a cultivated tree, and the cycads (order Cycadales) of the subtropics, the tropics, and the southern continental area. Cycads are often mistaken for palms because their stout, unbranched trunks are crowned by large pinnately compound leaves.

As rapidly as the gymnosperms replaced the older types of woody plants, the new reptiles replaced the old amphibians that had flourished during the latter half of the Carboniferous and early Permian. The scaly-skinned animals, with their eggs that could be laid on land, were much better adapted to repeated drought. So were the gymnosperms, as compared with the giant clubmosses and horsetail trees, whose reproduction depended upon sexual activity in delicate little gametophytes. Yet moisture and temperature can have been only part of the changing environment. In the seas, the trilobites and the jawless armored fishes disappeared—extinct after a history dating back more than 250 million years.

PLANTS OF MESOZOIC TIMES

Between the beginning of the Triassic period, which opened the Mesozoic era, and the end of the Cretaceous period, which closed it, lies the span of past time best known as the "Age of Reptiles." It encompasses the appearance, the flourishing and the disappearance of the dinosaurs, of the flying reptiles, of the porpoise-like ichthysaurs, of the sea-going plesiosaurs, and of others less popularly known. It saw the origin of the turtles, of the warm-blooded birds and mammals, of insects with a pupal stage, and of flowering plants. Initially the vegetation on the land included no generic group that has survived unchanged enough to bear the same name today. Late in the Cretaceous, a great many modern genera were well established and, except for the vertebrate animals that lived in the same habitats, the scene might have seemed as familiar as many at the present time. Among the vertebrates, no primate had yet evolved.

The Triassic and Jurassic periods had more kinds of gymnosperms than grew on the earth either before or subsequently.

Cycads, maidenhair trees, conifers, and members of two orders (Caytoniales and Cycadeoidales) that arose and disappeared during the Mesozoic, were the trees and shrubs. Below them grew ferns in large variety, small horsetails and clubmosses, mosses and liverworts. Actually, the earliest moss to be discovered in fossil form is of Jurassic age. Prior to the Cretaceous period, angiosperms (flowering plants) seem absent altogether, although their ancestors must have been present in small numbers. Pollen grains from coal of Jurassic age in Scotland are suspected of coming from some unknown form of vegetation related closely to buttercups and water lilies, but no other parts of the plant have been identified so far.

Probably the flowering plants evolved first in the Far North, perhaps well above the nearest pond or lagoon in which their parts could easily be fossilized. Many of the earliest known remains are of early Cretaceous age, from sedimentary rocks exposed in western Greenland. Until late in the period, no member of this important group of plants seems to have lived south of the Equator. Then they began displacing ferns and gymnosperms in the Southern Hemisphere.

After so long a history of unfamiliar, archaic plants, it seems strange to be encountering so many genera that have species alive today:

alder (*Alnus*)	laurel (*Laurus*)
birch (*Betula*)	magnolia (*Magnolia*)
breadfruit (*Artocarpus*)	persimmon (*Diosporos*)
buckthorn (*Rhamnus*)	sassafras (*Sassafras*)
chestnut (*Castanea*)	sycamore (*Platanus*)
custard-apple (*Annona*)	tulip tree (*Liriodendron*)
elm (*Ulmus*)	viburnum (*Viburnum*)
fig (*Ficus*)	walnut (*Juglans*)

Equally surprising is the number of these angiosperms, such as alder and birch, that are pollinated by wind rather than by insects. At least as important may be their ability to spread rapidly by sending up new stems from extended roots and to produce a whole tree from a branch that has been broken off and blown some distance by the wind.

All of the angiosperms in this list are woody plants of the subclass Dicotyledonae, which have two cotyledons (seed leaves) in the seed, just one vascular cylinder in the root and stem, leaves with netted veins, and flower parts in 4's or 5's or multiples (such as 8 or 10). Supposedly some nonwoody, herbaceous plants were present too, although evidence of these is almost completely lacking in the fossil record. A few monocotyledonous plants are known from the late Cretaceous, including the cabbage palm (*Sabal*), the greenbrier (*Smilax*) and a few representatives of the grass family and the water-plantain family. Like other "monocots" they have a single cotyledon in the seed, multiple vascular strands in the root and stem, leaves usually with unbranched veins extending from base (or midrib) to tip, and flower parts in 3's or multiples of 3; lacking a vascular cambium, they are never woody.

As we think about the land plants of the Mesozoic Era and the animals that fed on them (or on one another), we realize that ferns and gymnosperms were the principal diet available. No wonder so many of the herbivorous dinosaurs developed the habit still shown by many crocodilians and birds—swallowing pieces of rock which became embedded in the wall of the digestive tract and served as "gizzard stones" in grinding food. Certainly this rocky material added to the weight of the animals, and made it harder for them to be quick-moving.

During the Jurassic period, insects began a major diversification. Beetles, butterflies and moths, ants and bees and wasps appeared for the first time. All of these have a life history that includes a pupal stage. They are the types of insects that carry pollen from flower to flower while getting nourishment in the form of nectar and pollen. This mutually advantageous relationship could not evolve until ancestral plants and ancestral insects were ready simultaneously with matching adaptations. Probably the interaction developed slowly during the Jurassic, even though almost no fossil evidence for the existence of flowering plants has been found in rocks of this age. On the other hand Jurassic fossils do show the presence of these insects, and also of the first birds and mammals, all of which may have been insect-eaters.

Before the end of the Cretaceous period, the pollinating insects, the flowering plants, the birds and mammals had made an amazing start toward transforming the world of land life. Insect-pollinated plants replaced the wind-pollinated ones first in the tropics and subtropics. Herbaceous plants began attracting insects to flowers close to the ground, where wind pollination would be most unlikely. Flowering plants crowded the wind-pollinated gymnosperms into higher altitudes and higher latitudes. These changes continued, right up to the present time, through the millions of years known as the Cenozoic era.

PLANTS OF CENOZOIC TIMES

After about 170 million years with little mountain building and only sporadic volcanic activity, the earth began thrusting up new peaks early in the Cenozoic era. To some extent this may have been due to pressures caused by continental drift for, by the end of the Mesozoic Era, the large land masses seem to have reached almost their modern locations. The subcontinent of India crushed against the Eurasian continent, where the Himalayas and the Tibetan plateau rose high above sea level. The old connection between the eastern Indian Ocean and the Mediterranean Sea disappeared, making the old Tethys Sea unrecognizable. Antarctica and Australia began a long period of isolation. The spreading sea floor that was creating the Atlantic Oceans south and north moved the continents of the Western Hemisphere toward the Pacific Ocean. Near the west coast from Alaska to Tierra del Fuego an immense chain of mountains rose up—the Rockies and the Coast Range and the Andes.

Changing patterns in the animal life, particularly as early mammals were replaced by modern kinds, allow paleontologists to subdivide Cenozoic time. The replacement of Cretaceous vegetation with present types seems to have progressed more gradually through the first 61 of the 63 million years in the era. These are the years that are grouped under the historic name of the Tertiary, although the corresponding words, Primary for the Paleozoic and Secondary for the Mesozoic, have been dropped. The Quaternary is distinctly different, for it includes the Pleistocene (the "Ice Age") as a culmination of a long trend toward cooler temperatures, and the Recent (the last 15,000 years) which may be merely another interglacial opportunity for life to colonize higher latitudes and higher altitudes before great glaciers spread again.

The effects of the Ice Age show in the modern geographical distribution of plants. At each warming of the earth and melting back of the ice over the continents, vegetation has colonized the bare land. The pioneers have been gymnosperms such as spruce, fir and larch, or grasses and sedges, or small flowering plants of kinds that seem especially adapted to alpine conditions.

"LIVING FOSSILS" AND THREATS OF EXTINCTION

From the beginning of the fossil record to modern times, plants of newer kinds have replaced older types. At the same time, the variety of life has increased because plants have spread out of the seas into new habitats in fresh waters, then onto moist land, and presently to the edges of the ice and across the ultimate deserts. Sometimes it is possible to trace a genus or a species from its first appearance as a fossil to an understandable end.

The genus *Ginkgo* appears first among fossils of the Jurassic period, as one of many in the order Ginkgoales at the time. Alone it represented this order through the Cenozoic. Only one species, the maidenhair tree (*G. biloba*), is known to have been a contemporary of mankind. It was native to the Far East, and there attracted the attention of Buddhist monks who began cultivating it as an unusual shade tree with fan-shaped leaves. Travelers from Europe discovered it in temple courtyards, and introduced it elsewhere. But explorers have

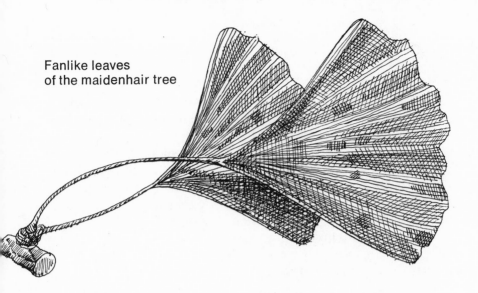

Fanlike leaves
of the maidenhair tree

been able to find no native groves of *Ginkgo* anywhere. Apparently it was a "living fossil," with no surviving close relatives, and became extinct except for the trees propagated as a curiosity.

The "dawn redwood" (*Metasequoia*) was discovered first as fossilized remains in Cretaceous rocks, and then as a small grove in western China where woodcutters were cutting every tree of useful size. Poor communications hide the present state of this one small grove. But samples of the dawn redwood are now reproducing in botanic gardens and on private estates in many countries. The "living fossil" seems safe from extinction for the moment, but only through human intervention.

The American botanist William Bartram of Philadelphia collected some cuttings of a tree new to him in the valley of the Altamaha River in Georgia. When it proved to be new to science also, he gave it the name *Franklinia alatamaha* to honor Benjamin Franklin. But on subsequent trips to the same part of Georgia and elsewhere, neither Bartram nor any other plantsman has yet found this tree growing naturally. It vanished, became extinct in the wild, with no known cause beyond the fact that it did not compete successfully with other vegetation. Now placed in the same genus as the tea tree and known popularly as the "Lost *Camellia*," this plant could easily have disappeared without anyone knowing of its existence. Like the ginkgo and the dawn redwood, it was rescued at the last moment and given another lease on life in a new and protected habitat.

The ecologist refers to this replacement of old species by new ones as the outcome of "competitive exclusion." It can also take place because of a sudden change in the habitat. Today, more native plants in the world are threatened by man-made changes in the habitat than by natural forces of competitive exclusion.

HOW DID IT ALL BEGIN?

So far as anyone has been able to demonstrate in the field or the laboratory, the plants that are alive today are the ancestors of all future members of the Plant Kingdom. No plant or animal or microbe originates from any mixture of organic and inorganic materials. Only life can organize materials to produce more life.

This conclusion challenges the scientist to find a logical exception in the past and account for the origin of life on earth by natural (rather than supernatural) processes. How could life originate spontaneously during the early Pre-Cambrian Era and not today? A Russian scientist, A. E. Oparin, suggested in 1938 that the change in the environment may have been as simple as an oxygen-free atmosphere in the early history of the earth, and then one with oxygen when green plants evolved and began releasing the gas through photosynthesis. Without oxygen to combine with inorganic and organic compounds, the substances that would remain unchanged in sea water would be quite different. Ions containing either phosphorus or nitrogen would be far more numerous. Amino acids, nucleotides and other organic compounds would not be oxidized and destroyed spontaneously. If any natural processes could produce these materials, they might accumulate to modest concentrations, particularly in tide pools where sunlight could evaporate some of the water.

In 1953 at the University of Chicago and with advice from

Nobel laureate Harold C. Urey, a young biochemist (Stanley
L. Miller) built a piece of glassware in which he could im-
prison an artificial atmosphere containing the gases nitrogen,
ammonia, carbon monoxide, carbon dioxide, methane, water
and free hydrogen. With heat he provided a continual circu-
lation of these materials through water and past an electric
spark to simulate lightning during Pre-Cambrian storms. Within a week, these ingredients reacted and formed several
different amino acids in milligram amounts. His discovery was
repeated, with variations, by many other scientists, using
different proportions of the same gases. In each case, amino
acids arose without any living thing to carry on the synthesis.

Later experimenters added inorganic compounds of
phosphorus to the simple brew and found among the spontaneous products the nucleotide ATP (adenosine triphosphate), which is the energy carrier in most chemical
reactions of living cells. Apparently the most essential building
blocks for proteins, nucleic acids, and perhaps lipids too could
arise by natural processes. How much more would be needed
to create a virus, or a cell membrane, or the simplest living
cell that could be imagined?

So far as is known, no virus can reproduce without a living
cell to do the work. That cell comes first—not the parasitic
virus. And the cell must have all of the exquisite organelles
and special membranes required for selectively absorbing
raw materials, for facilitating their interaction in perhaps a
minimum of 40 different syntheses, for regulating these activities in sequence, for replicating its DNA and moving a
replica into the far end of a daughter cell as the old one
divides in two. No one has discovered yet how many hundreds
of millions of years intervened between the beginning of
chemical evolution and the unlikely (although statistically
possible) coincidence that gave the characteristics of life to
an organized mass of materials within a membrane. Nor is it
known how much further time went by before diversification
by mutation and natural selection produced a cell in which
the addition of chlorophyll gave access to a new source of

energy—sunlight freshly absorbed. Until that point, all* life must have nourished itself on organic compounds from the water or from another mote of life. The process of spontaneous generation could continue. But with oxygen from photosynthesis to release the energy from organic compounds before living things could absorb these materials, life from pre-existing life would soon become the only way.

* A few exceptions can be found. Known as autotrophic bacteria, they get energy for life by simplifying hydrogen sulfide, releasing free sulfur; or by oxidizing free sulfur to sulfuric acid; or by utilizing both sulfuric acid and iron sulfate to produce as a final product "bog iron ore," which is called limonite. Still different bacteria can absorb sulfuric acid and petroleum, then get their energy while ridding themselves of hydrogen sulfide and water. Although rarely noticed, these forms of life demonstrate the possibility of other systems on which life can maintain itself and reproduce.

9

The Spread of Plant Life

In 1964, the people of Great Britain celebrated the 400th anniversary of the birth of William Shakespeare. In the same year, the delegates to the Twentieth International Congress of Botany met in Great Britain. Many of the botanists from all over the world made a side trip to Stratford-on-Avon to enjoy the Shakespeare Festival. Many of them visited the famous garden of Shakespeare's wife, Anne Hathaway. A good many of these experienced plantsmen looked at the spectacular display of flowers in the garden and began to protest to one another: "But . . . But . . . But. . . !" They knew that many of these plants were unknown in England during Shakespeare's day.

> Tall goldenrods from North America
> Tall dahlias from Mexico
> Showy gaillardias from the American plains
> "French" marigolds from Argentina
> Scarlet Salvia from Brazil

Four hundred years ago the potato and the tomato were

unknown in Britain. No European had yet seen a eucalyptus tree. In fact, so little was familiar regarding plants from distant lands that the problem of classifying them had not arisen.

The world of plants became a fascinating aspect of geography in much more recent times. It gathered this appeal chiefly through the deductions of three men. Two of them were Germans who traveled widely, and the third an Englishman who stayed close to home.

The first German was a naturalist who spent five years intensively exploring South America, taking copious notes, collecting specimens, and then 30 years in writing up his discoveries in 30 fact-filled volumes. This outstanding naturalist is generally known as Alexander von Humboldt, although his full name was Friedrich Heinrich Alexander, Freiherr von Humboldt. Accompanied by the French botanist Aimé Bonpland, he arrived in Caracas (now in Venezuela) in 1799 and soon set out to explore the Orinoco River system. He confirmed its connection with the Amazon, and studied the life of the rain forests and savannas that paralleled the river channels. Traveling was difficult, for only primitive canoes were available on the upper reaches of the river.

Von Humboldt and his friend took a short holiday in Cuba, but could not resist examining the native plants on this westernmost island of the West Indies. Then the two set off again for Cartagena, Colombia, and a hazardous trip overland along the mountain chains through Ecuador to the coast of Peru. There von Humboldt measured the temperature of the offshore waters, noticed the direction of water movement, and correctly interpreted the unusual chill to indicate that a northbound current (now known as the Humboldt) reached equatorial latitudes all the way from cold Antarctic regions.

By ship, von Humboldt and Bonpland traveled to Mexico, where they explored for a year, then visited several parts of the United States, and returned to Paris in 1804, loaded down with notes and preserved specimens. The following year the first of the 30 volumes entitled *Voyages of Humboldt and Bonpland* was published. Volume 5 included the first comprehensive account of plant geography. A later volume, in 1817, introduced an invention of von Humboldt's: maps with lines drawn to connect places with the same temperature. Isotherms have since become the familiar way to compare weather conditions in different regions.

The second German, the botanist Andreas Franz Wilhelm Schimper, began his botanical explorations with two separate trips to the West Indies (1881, 1882–83), and one to Brazil (1886). Then he turned to the eastern tropics in Ceylon and Java (1889–90) and traveled as a member of the scientific crew aboard the *Valdivia* deep-sea expedition (1898–99) to the Canary Islands, the Cameroons, East Africa, the Seychelles, and Sumatra. No naturalist before him had ever seen so many parts of the tropics. Yet Schimper found time to compile his observations and conclusions into an influential book (1898),which was promptly translated into English as *Plant Geography Upon a Physiological Basis*. Upon his death, other botanists revised and enlarged it in 1903; in this form, as a classic, it was reprinted in 1964. Today the first part of Schimper's book can be recognized as a good grasp of ecology; the second part concerns the geographical distribution of plants; the final third presents a clear classification of all the plants the author knew. No wonder the book in its original edition is 876 pages long.

Professor Ronald Good has had less need to travel. In the great botanic garden at Kew near London, and in the city's magnificent museums full of plants from all over the world, he has been able to concentrate on finding patterns in the distribution of angiosperms. Twice he has revised his book *The Geography of the Flowering Plants* (1947), most recently in 1964. Changes were made necessary by new discoveries by plant explorers in remote parts of the world.

Both plants and animals live where they do because conditions are suitable, because their ancestors evolved there or reached the region by travel in understandable ways from some other place. Consequently, the fundamental pattern on the continents might be expected to be similar for all kinds of

The geographic kingdoms of land plants

BOREAL KINGDOM

PALEOTROPICAL KINGDOM

AUSTRALIAN KINGDOM

CAPE KINGDOM

NEOTROPICAL KINGDOM

ANTARCTIC KINGDOM

life. Generally it is. But the inability of plants to fly against prevailing winds, to swim across currents through narrow straits, to be active as birds and mammals are when the temperature is below freezing, introduces some differences in distribution. The dependence of some kinds of flowering plants upon suitable animals to carry their pollen or transport their seeds has limited their reproduction and their range.

Today, plant geographers focus their attention mostly on the angiosperms, despite the fact that this class became conspicuous only in the Cretaceous period 135 million years ago, as compared to at least 400 million years for some other classes of vascular plants. This may be justified by the fact that angiosperms include more than 250,000 species, of which 200,000 are dicots. By contrast, the gymnosperms and all other vascular plants number fewer than 11,000 species. Terrestrial thallophytes—principally fungi and lichens—have fewer than 77,000 representatives, and bryophytes about 23,000.

The geography of flowering plants shows six subdivisions which differ greatly in size. By far the largest is the "boreal kingdom," which includes most of North America, all of Europe, North Africa and coastal Asia Minor, and Asia north of the Himalayas to the coast of the China Sea near Shanghai. Next in size is the "paleotropical kingdom," with the rest of Africa (except its southern tip), the Arabian peninsula, Pakistan and India, the Malay Peninsula and Southeast Asia, plus the East Indies, the Philippines, New Guinea and most of the islands of the Pacific as far as Hawaii and French Polynesia. A corresponding "neotropical kingdom" includes coastal and southern Mexico, Central America, the West Indies and the Bahamas, the tip of Florida, and all of South America except its southern end. Australia, with Tasmania, is a separate "kingdom." A scattered "antarctic kingdom" includes the tip of South America, the oceanic islands of the South Temperate Zone, and New Zealand; in the past its plants lived along the coasts of Antarctica as well. Smallest of all is the "Cape kingdom" at the tip of South Africa.

In each of these "kingdoms" of plant geography, an impressive number of plant families, genera and species are native that are found nowhere else. Referred to as endemics, they confer botanical character upon the floral subdivision.

Most of this pattern shown by the flowering plants matches quite well the geographical distribution of animal life. The boreal kingdom of the phytogeographer would be called the holarctic realm by zoogeographers; they would use the same terms paleotropical and neotropical for corresponding areas, but include New Guinea with Australia in an Australasian realm. Until recently they have lumped New Zealand with Australia, without realizing that its true affinities are more with Antarctica and with islands such as New Caledonia to the north. But no features of the Cape region of South Africa would lead a zoologist to follow the botanists in recognizing it as distinctive. Since the flowering plants and the animals correspond as well as they do in their distribution, it seems likely that the other vascular plants, the bryophytes and terrestrial thallophytes do too.

PLANTS OF THE BOREAL KINGDOM

Named for Boreas, the Greek god of the north wind, this vast area with similar plants includes most of the continental areas derived from the old supercontinent of Laurasia. Its unifying features began in Paleozoic times, before spreading of the sea floor separated North America from Europe and created the North Atlantic Ocean. But as the New World moved away from the Old World along the Atlantic, it moved closer in the Pacific. A land bridge formed between Alaska and Siberia at many times during the Cenozoic era, allowing emigrations in both directions where now the Bering Strait provides a barrier. Four times during the Ice Age, immense glaciers in the north and on major mountains spread during cooler weather, and forced every plant species either to shift its range into warmer areas or be obliterated. Most of them shifted south and down the mountain slopes, and then, when interglacial times arrived, they moved back again. Each move

Old-style flowers of magnolia and tulip tree

decreased their variety to some extent. But with each return to higher latitudes and higher altitudes, they were accompanied by some extra colonists from the tropics. These combinations provided the flora of the boreal kingdom as it is seen today.

The boreal is such a large region and familiar to so many people that the list of its distinctive plants is long. It harbors all or almost all of the world's poplars, hornbeams, hazels, birches, beeches, chestnuts, magnolias, tulip trees, true laurels, witch hazels, sycamores, spiraeas, maples (a few live in Java and Sumatra), basswoods (lindens), fireweeds, wintergreens, primroses, ash trees, forget-me-nots and honeysuckles. It has also all, or nearly all, of the known kinds of yews, spruces, hemlocks, Douglas firs, true firs and larches. Pines could be added to this list if they had not spread down the mountain chains in the New World into Central America, and hence into the neotropical kingdom.

Often the boreal kingdom is subdivided into floral provinces. Farthest north is a circumpolar arctic-subarctic province of tundra plants. It extends across northern Alaska, northern Canada, includes all of Greenland and Iceland, northern Scandinavia and the northern U.S.S.R. South of this in the New World are two unequal provinces. The Pacific North American province, which is largely forested, includes southernmost Alaska, British Columbia, the mountainous parts of the Yukon Territory and of Alberta, then southward just west of the Great Plains all the way to the boundary of the neotropical kingdom. The rest of Alaska, the Yukon, Canada and the continental United States except the tip of Florida composes an Atlantic North American province. It has spruce-fir taiga in the north, great grasslands in the western two-thirds, and formerly had an extensive deciduous forest in the northeast and a mixed hardwood and coniferous forest in the southeast. These North American provinces are the native home of almost all goldenrods and sunflowers. The Atlantic North American province provided the world with Virginia creeper, as a close relative to "Boston" ivy—from China and Japan.

Correspondingly in Eurasia, the vast area south of the arctic-subarctic province can be subdivided rather easily into

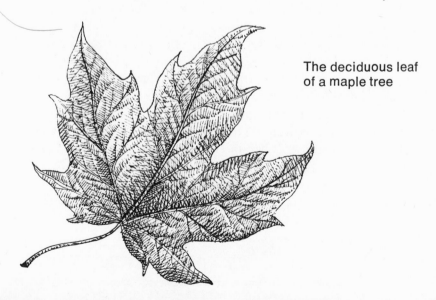

The deciduous leaf
of a maple tree

five parts. Largest is an east-west band the southern boundary
of which crosses northern Spain, stays just north of the
Mediterranean, follows the Caucasus Mountains to the eastern
shore of the Caspian Sea, curves northward and westward to
the Crimean Peninsula, then north and east across Asia to the
Pacific Ocean just north of Japan. The northern portion of this
Euro-Siberian province is still clad in a taiga of spruce, fir and
larch. In the western portions are many remnants of the former
deciduous forests of oak and beech. Farther east, where the
climate is too dry to support the forest of the taiga, are grasslands and semi-deserts. South of this province in the far west
is the Macaronesian province including the Azores, Madeira,
the Canary Islands, and the Cape Verde Islands off the west
coast of Africa. Their plants seem to have come to them in
wind storms and as rafted vegetation on oceanic currents from
Europe more than from Africa. Yet in their isolation the plants
have evolved unique ways of life. Madeira has a member of
the carrot family that attains tree size and is found nowhere
else. This island shares three local genera of plants with the
Canaries, and another with both the Canaries and the Azores.
The Cape Verdes have two plant genera of their own.

The Mediterranean province around the coasts of this great
sea was formerly forested with oaks and pines, but centuries
of careless lumbering, burning, and unrestricted grazing have
converted it into barren lands whose soil often seems merely
crumbled rock. The old olive trees that survive there sometimes are the remnants of orchards the Romans established.
The grapes on the hillsides are still under cultivation after
unknown lengths of time. But in places, particularly on the
African coast in the western parts of the province, forests of
ancient cork oaks relieve a landscape that is more often
dominated by woody shrubs interlaced with thorny vines. This
is the home of the pomegranate, of alfalfa, of English daisies,
of gorse and mullein. In it many of the favorite herbs, such as
lavender, thyme and rosemary grow wild as they have for
millenia.

The western and central Asiatic province encompasses a

whole series of deserts, from the Iranian to the Gobi. Bitterly cold winters alternate with intense summer heat, and an average rainfall of usually less than 6 inches. Saltbush and saxual grow where the soil is salty, and the saxual almost alone where the chronic drought matches poor, sandy land. Surrounding these deserts are grasslands, some of which surprisingly support tulips, hyacinths, and other familiar garden flowers of early spring, which here are on their native territory. So are rhubarb, spinach, and hemp.

More kinds of trees live today in the Sino-Japanese province than in all of the other provinces of the boreal kingdom combined. The area includes many of the forested slopes of the Himalayas, from which horticulturalists all over the temperate world have introduced rhododendrons and other shrubs with handsome flowers and foliage. This province is the home of the nandina bush, the forsythias, white mulberries, Chinese elms and Japanese magnolias.

A surprising number of trees and herbs in these areas of Japan and China belong to the same genera as species that are native to the Atlantic North American province. The ginsengs, the magnolias and the tulip trees, the trailing arbutus and partridgeberry are to be found in both provinces. They retain this distribution from Pliocene times, when a warmer and moister climate around the northern end of the Pacific Ocean and a broad land bridge where the Bering Strait is now allowed an interchange between Alaska and Siberia, and southward in both the New World and the Old. For a while a forested corridor connected the Sino-Japanese province to the Atlantic North American province by way of central Alaska. Despite later shifts in vegetation due to the immense glaciers of the Ice Age, this past history left Canada with enough maples to provide a national emblem, and left Japan with more than twice as many of this familiar type of tree.

PLANTS OF THE PALEOTROPICAL KINGDOM

Two of the three parts of the paleotropical kingdom are conspicuously separated by the Indian Ocean. An almost

north-south line just west of Delhi separates the African subkingdom to the west from the Indo-Malaysian subkingdom to
the east. The line is also the eastern boundary of a great North
African-Indian desert province that stretches westward to the
Atlantic coast and includes the Great Indian Desert, the
Arabian deserts, and the vast Sahara. It is best known for its
oases of date palms, and its scattered low trees yielding
fragrant gums called frankincense and myrrh. To the south in
Africa are separate provinces from east to west: the Madagascan, the East African, the West African rain forest, and in the
South Atlantic another province for Ascension and St. Helena
Islands. South of these is a South African province that does
not include the Cape area.

The Madagascan province includes the remote islands of
the Indian Ocean, such as the Comoros, the Mascarenes and
the Seychelles. On the Seychelles is the famous coco de mer
or double coconut palm, with the largest fruits in the world.
Madagascar is rich in palms, but also is the home of the
traveler's-tree, the royal poinciana, and the dragon-tree—
source of the "dragon's-blood" resin used in photoengraving
and for musical instruments. The East African province is
mostly a high savanna, with great expanses of elephant grass,
scattered flat-topped acacia trees, and grotesquely bulky
baobab trees. It supports more kinds of cud-chewing mammals
and other spectacular animals than any other part of the
modern world. The West African rain forest is mostly in the
basin of the Congo River and along the coast to the west and
north. It is the home of the African oil palm, Senegal ma-
hogany, Liberian coffee, and a tree called akee with a bright
orange fruit containing delicious inner parts that are poisonous
except for a brief period—just a few days—at the peak of
ripeness. The Atlantic islands form a special province because
their plants show affinities to those of both Africa and South
America; none are widely known. By contrast, the South
African province is dominated by the semiarid lands called
the karroo and by the Kalahari Desert of Botswana and the
Namib Desert of South West Africa. Its plants include many

succulents that are similar to cacti without being cacti. The strangest, called stone plants because they resemble smooth pebbles, belong to the carpetweed family, just as the fig marigolds or ice plants (*Mesembrythemum*) do; the latter have been introduced in many parts of the world as a ground cover where frost is not severe. Other succulents are mostly spiny aloes of the lily family, spiny spurges, carrion-flowers (*Stapelia*) of the milkweed family, or thick-leaved crassulas and related plants of the orpine family. The degree to which similar environmental conditions have selected matching adaptations in vegetation of unrelated families is the most impressive feature.

Much of the original exploration of the Indo-Malaysian subkingdom was done by European captains who took their ships around the southern tip of Africa in search of cheaper and more reliable ways to obtain spices from the East. The alternative to these long journeys was reliance upon camel caravans threading across the deserts of the North African–Indian desert province. Led by Arab traders, the plodding beasts could never bring enough to satisfy the demands in Europe.

In Asia, an Indian province includes Assam, but is distinct from a Continental Southeast Asiatic province (including the island of Formosa), and from a Malaysian province extending to the tip of the Malay peninsula and encompassing all of the East Indies, the Philippines and New Guinea. The Indian province is a realm of sandalwood trees, and bananas of many varieties. It is also the home of jute, indigo, cinnamon, pepper, sesame, and the wine palm, of mangoes, cucumbers, eggplant and banyan trees. The Southeast Asiatic province is the source of the camphor tree, the purple orchid tree, the ginger lily, the "Cape" jasmine and crepe myrtle. The Malaysian is best known for its giant bamboos, sago palms, taro, breadfruits and crotons. Originally limited to this province were spice ginger, cloves, nutmeg and mace.

Beyond these subkingdoms in the Pacific ocean is a Polynesian subkingdom of the paleotropical, extending to Hawaii and Tahiti. It includes the home of the Norfolk Island "pine," which is widely used as a decorative tree, and in Hawaii of the strange members of the daisy family known as silverswords and greenswords, which produce a towering cluster of flowers only once, at the end of a long life.

PLANTS OF THE NEOTROPICAL KINGDOM

Until less than 25 million years ago, this part of the Western World was cut off for immensities of time from North America, and separated by broad straits into an island area of Central America and the West Indies and a distinct South American continent. Neither plants nor animals had much opportunity to cross the open water and colonize beyond. Now a land bridge links the northern continent to Central America and another to South America. The first part, at the isthmus of Tehuantepec in Mexico, is so low that it would be flooded by any major rise in sea level. The second, at the isthmus of Panama, has a narrow ridge of eroding volcanoes that separate the waters of the Pacific Ocean from those of the Caribbean Sea and Atlantic Ocean by less than 40 miles.

For at least 50 million years, the spectacular Andes Mountains have divided South America into a narrow, steep western slope and a broad eastern one. Trade winds from the east drive an equatorial current across the South Atlantic, where it splits into a southbound portion that warms the coast of the continent to the latitude of Buenos Aires, and a northbound portion that continues around the shores of the Caribbean and the Gulf of Mexico, then forces warm water out between Florida and Cuba as the Gulf Stream. Meanwhile the trade winds continue westward up the sloping land, dropping moisture into the vast basin shared by the Amazon River and the Orinoco. This nourishes the largest rain forest in the world, concealing cacao and Pará rubber trees, Brazil nuts, and the giant among water lilies.

The westerly winds farther south, produced by the rotation of the earth, propel ocean waters eastward in the "roaring Forties." Some of this current turns south to pass between the tip of South America and Antarctica, but much of it turns north, instead, to become the cold Humboldt current. It diminishes the potential rainfall along the west coast all the way to the Equator. Together, the Andes, the prevailing winds and the Humboldt current produce the driest deserts in the world within sight of the Pacific Ocean, in Chile and Peru. They create a semiarid grasslands at high elevation, called the altiplano through parts of Peru and Bolivia. Yet from vegetation native to this isolated habitat have come both the potato and the tomato, each developed to much larger size by horticulturalists.

The neotropical kingdom is the principal native home of cacti and century plants. Its endemics include cabbage palms, royal palms and wax palms, the avocado and papaya, cannas and nasturtiums, the coca tree from which cocaine is obtained, the cinchona tree that is the source of quinine, the tobacco plant, the cacao tree whose seeds ("cocoa beans") yield chocolate, and the climbing orchid whose fruits ("vanilla beans") yield natural vanilla flavoring. The pineapple comes from a neotropical family called the bromeliads, many of which live as perching plants (epiphytes) on the outstretched limbs of great trees in the rain forests.

Careful attention to details of plant geography in the neotropical kingdom leads to recognition of a Caribbean province which extends also across northern South America; a Venezuelan-Guianian province between the mouth of the Orinoco and that of the Amazon; the great Amazonian province; a South Brazilian province that is seasonally much drier; a Pampas province, where the vegetation is a natural grassland from Paraguay south far into Argentina; and a small special province off the Chilean coast for the Juan Fernandez Islands. The Juan Fernandez, one of which is the fictional site of the story of Robinson Crusoe, have plants that arrived long ago from both directions—westward across the Humboldt current from South America, and eastward across the wide Pacific Ocean from islands of Polynesia.

PLANTS OF THE AUSTRALIAN KINGDOM

One genus of plants (*Eucalyptus*) in the myrtle family distinguishes the flora of Australia more than any other. In almost all parts of the continent where trees of any kind will grow, members of this genus are found. The 600 species are known by many names, most often as gums. By natural means they have spread beyond the continental limits into some parts of New Guinea and the East Indies. Australian species include a giant called "mountain ash," which grows to be as much as 326 feet tall and 25 feet in diameter at the height of a man's chest. By contrast, mallee is a dwarf eucalypt that dominates an extensive scrubland along the fringe of Australia's vast deserts. Dwarf acacias of the pea family, particularly one called mulga, form a different scrubland that formerly covered nearly 30 percent of the continent. Of the world's acacias, about 600 species grow in Australia, and 200 in all other countries combined.

The bottlebrush trees and the cajeput (or punkbark) tree have been introduced to other parts of the world. Plantations of *Macadamia* trees have been set out in Hawaii to produce macadamia (or Queensland) nuts as popular snacks. "Australian pines" are members of a distinctive family of flowering trees, now used elsewhere as windbreaks. Their leaves are minute, scalelike, and borne inconspicuously in whorls around the joints of green twigs, for which the plant is also called a "horsetail tree." Australians know their species of the genus (*Casuarina*) as beefwoods because of the blood-red color of the heartwood, or as she-oaks from the hardness of the wood and the soft "shee-ing" sound of a breeze through the green branches. A few of the 50 species have extended their range into New Caledonia and also westward through the East Indies to the Mascarene Islands in the Indian Ocean.

Other distinctive plants of the Australian flora bear names adopted from the aborigines, such as karri, jarrah, wandoo and coolibah (all eucalypts), waratah and lillypilly. A few are more descriptive, without indicating real relationships:

kangaroo-paws, grasstrees, bastard box, Australian tea-trees, stringy barks and iron-barks.

PLANTS OF THE ANTARCTIC KINGDOM

The winds of the "Roaring Forties" seem to have propelled many plants to new landfalls around the southern latitudes. While the climate was warmer and vegetation grew along the coasts of Antarctica, this transportation system probably operated more efficiently than it does today. It is believed to account for the forests of antarctic beech in the Patagonian province at the tip of South America, on the South Island of New Zealand (a country constituting the New Zealand province), and of Tasmania and the mountains of eastern Australia along which it has spread to the highlands of New Guinea. Fossils of antarctic beech are known from Antarctica itself.

This same distribution, with some especially distinctive outliers in the Cape floral kingdom of South Africa, is shown by members of the strange protea family. One, known as honeysuckle, is New Zealand's only kind of deciduous tree. In Australia, its near relatives include among the eucalyptus forests handsome shrubs with large flowers known as Australian honeysuckles, five different *Macadamia* trees, and a strange shrub known as wooden pears because of its pear-shaped, inedible woody fruits. The Australian silky-oak is another member of this family; it has been introduced into the southern United States as a shade tree yielding valuable timber. Of the 1,200 species in the protea family, 700 live in Australia, 475 in South Africa, 1 in New Zealand, and 24 in southernmost South America.

Today, the cool climate that maintains the vast ice cap on Antarctica also prevents trees from growing on most of the oceanic islands in the South Temperate Zone. Antarctic grasses and strange members of the cabbage family are native to these isolated, wind-swept points of land, making them so inhospitable to people and domestic animals that even the names of the islands are seldom heard: the South Orkneys,

South Georgia, South Sandwich, Bouvet, Crozet, Kerguelen, Heard, Macquarie, Auckland, Campbell, Bounty, Chatham, and the Antipodes. The Falkland Islands off the tip of Tierra del Feugo are included in the Patagonian province, although more of their flora and fauna have come from adjacent South America.

PLANTS OF THE CAPE FLORAL KINGDOM

Isolated for millions of years from any temperate avenue for overland propagation, the plants at the cool moist tip of South Africa have had a long period in which to diversify. North of them are arid lands, such as the dreaded Namib Desert along the coast of South West Africa, and the rolling grasslands of the South African karroo. With insects and sunbirds as pollinators, they have evolved a special wealth of flowering herbs, shrubs and trees. From this flora the horticulturalists of other countries have obtained the calla lily, the Cape tulip (or blood lily), the belladonna lily (*Amaryllis*), the "African" lily (*Agapanthus*), the "Guernsey" lily (*Nerine*), the Cape cowslips (*Lachenalia*), freesias, and the brilliantly colorful Namaqualand daisies.

Less promptly appreciated were the extraordinarily slow-growing hardwood trees, such as stinkwood, which were harvested for furniture- and cabinet-making until almost exterminated. Cliffs are often clad in a remarkable variety among the shrubby heaths (*Erica*), which grow otherwise mostly in the Mediterranean province and the north of Europe. Together with harsh woody members of the protea family, the heaths form thickets that are extremely difficult to penetrate. On various of the proteas, the flowers have such unusual forms that a layman can appreciate the choice of the name *Protea*, from that of the Greek god Proteus, who was famous for assuming a multitude of disguises. Among members of this family is the famous silvertree of Table Mountain, whose narrow leaves resemble those of willow except for their dry texture and feltlike covering of fine silky hair.

10
Plants and Mankind

At Qalat Jarmo in northeastern Iraq, archeologists have unearthed the remains of an exceedingly ancient human community. The lowest, oldest levels include samples of wheat, cultivated barley, and bones of dog and goat. Using the radiocarbon technique, a date has been assigned to these: 6750 B.C., nearly 9,000 years before the present. Yet among these pieces of waste from food are flint sickle blades and milling stones, showing that already man had made great strides in handling the grains of cereal grasses. Higher, more recent levels in this old community include fragments of the first known pottery.

From other sites in the Near East and elsewhere, the evidence seems consistent. It indicates that man's deliberate reliance upon plants began around 12,000 years ago in Asia Minor. This development of agriculture added something new, of immense importance, to the old knowledge of which wild plants (and animals) were good to eat. It gave mankind the ability to carry seeds and appropriate stone tools to new areas in the wilderness and there improve upon the familiar way of life.

The most astonishing feature in this prehistory of mankind is that almost the only plants to be domesticated for several thousand years were kinds native to Asia Minor. There, particularly in the valley between the Tigris and Euphrates Rivers and around the eastern end of the Mediterranean and up the Nile River, civilizations developed. Each was possible only because plant crops provided a more reliable supply of food—in greater abundance than could be obtained by the most skilled gatherers of wild edible roots, stems, leaves, fruits and seeds.

Much later, the primitive food gatherers and hunters who had spread across Asia and into the New World discovered the maize plant, and beans, and various kinds of edible gourds, such as squash and pumpkin. When the Spanish began exploring in tropical America, they found the Indians raising these foods in quantities large enough to supply the

Fruit clusters
("ears") of maize

residents of cities. The old Inca and Aztec civilizations were based upon maize ("Indian corn") and beans. Similarly, in the river valleys of China, other members of the mongoloid racial group learned to cultivate native rice in irrigated paddy fields. Upon this food supply, they too developed a great cultural heritage.

When we think about it, we realize how fundamental the cultivated plants have been in the changing fortunes of peoples on the various continents. The Pilgrim Fathers who came to settle the New England states in the 1600's did not have to explore for edible plants, or accustom themselves to the strange diet of native Indian tribes. Instead, they brought from Europe the living seeds of wheat, barley, oats and rye, of carrot, turnip, beet and onion, of cabbage and garden pea. They introduced the Old World apple, pear and plum, the gooseberry and currant, flax and cotton. Later they adopted the maize, the beans and gourds of the Indians, and still later obtained by way of Europe some improved strains of potatoes —starchy swellings on the subterranean stems of plants native to the high Andes.

Survival for the colonists in America depended upon protecting crops until they could mature and be harvested. Although the Indians tried desperately to destroy the foreign invaders, burning the food that the settlers had stored for winter use and all of their possessions too, competition between Indian and white was never on an equal basis. The colonists never had to live off the land and fight with Indian weapons. The settlers always had the better guns with which to protect their European way of life. Progressively they extended their hold on the continent.

When the Mormon pioneers reached the site of Salt Lake City in 1847, they had seeds to sow as well as food to last until the crops would ripen. But a hazard of the wilderness appeared just as the first wheat began to ripen: wingless crickets in great numbers. The insects destroyed much of the crop, and seemed about to finish it—leaving the Mormon pioneers none to eat during the coming winter. Then "sea gulls" arrived from adjacent lake shores and gobbled up the crickets. Gratefully the Mormons harvested what was left of their wheat, and erected a monument to the birds that had rescued them from sure starvation. After all, what native plants grew in the Salt Lake City area of Utah upon which people could live in European style during the cold months? No one then had any answer.

Within the last 300 years, peoples with a tradition of agriculture have swiftly displaced other peoples who resisted acquiring these customs. The Pygmies of African forests and the Hottentots and Bushmen of more open country lost their territories and almost vanished as agricultural tribesmen extended their plantations of millet, sorghum and wheat, and more recently of the maize they know as "mealies." The Australian aborigines retired away from the best agricultural land on their continent as pioneers introduced wheat, potatoes and pasture grasses to support a European way of life.

USEFUL PLANTS

In most parts of the world, people eat foods of plant origin as the staple feature in their diet. These plant products may come from roots, or stems, or leaves, or fruits. But they provide the bulk in the meal, and most of the energy—the calories that the dietitian counts. To a large extent, this is true because plant foods are easier to raise and to store than meat animals. A person can live on a completely vegetarian diet, even without eggs or milk. Yet in the Far North, where plant foods are unavailable to Eskimos in winter, these people subsist on meat alone. Equally exceptional are the tribesmen in equatorial Africa who live on a traditional mixture of cow's blood and milk. As nomads with their herds they move too frequently to make use of plant crops of any kind.

Almost two-thirds of humanity relies on polished white rice as the principal source of calories. Rice grows well only in warm countries, where it can be supplied with fresh or slightly brackish water in abundance. Unfortunately, although the area that is suited to rice culture is relatively small, the number of people wanting rice to eat grows faster than populations that rely upon other grains.

To make rice edible, it needs to be boiled for only a short time in a little water. No expensive equipment is necessary. Dry grass or rice stalks can serve as fuel. Furthermore, hand labor can substitute for machines in raising rice productively. Under suitable conditions of culture, it also yields more food per square mile than any other plant—enough to supply the needs of 1,538 people for a year. On the other hand, neither man nor animal can live long on polished white rice alone, no matter how it is cooked. In this form, which is preferred by rice eaters, the food is seriously deficient in vitamins and proteins. These must be added to the meal as extra vegetables with, preferably, some fish or meat. People who cannot afford to supplement their rice in this way may feel full, and get enough calories, yet still be malnourished.

Wheat is second only to rice as a nourishing food. Its great advantage is that it grows well on natural grasslands, without irrigation, and needs a minimum of moisture. The world has far more area suitable for raising wheat than for rice, or for any other plants that yield an abundance of nutritious carbohydrates. But to be prepared for eating, wheat grains must be ground to a fine flour. Then the flour must be cooked skillfully, perhaps in bread dough. All of this requires machinery, perhaps an oven, and fuel. Many parts of the world lack the equipment and the fuel with which to make wheat edible.

Among the starchy, staple foods, potatoes are unique. They are neither grasses nor fruits from flowers. Instead, a potato is a tuberous swelling on the underground stems of the potato plant, as a center in which starch is stored. The "eyes" of a potato are buds, and a piece of a potato with an "eye" can be used in place of a seed to initiate the growth of a new potato plant.

In the mountains of their native Peru, potato plants seldom get enough water or fertilizer. A yield of 3 million pounds of potatoes per square mile is considered normal. But in Ireland, the Netherlands and Poland, where irrigation water and ferti-

Flowers, fruit, foliage, and tuber of a potato

lizer are added in more scientific culture of potato plants, any less than 13 million pounds of potatoes per square mile would be regarded as a poor crop.

The cultivation of potato plants and the eating of potatoes as the principal starchy food in the diet began in Ireland late in the seventeenth century. This "vegetable" became famous as "Irish" potatoes. Actually, the greatest benefit in those troubled times was that the potatoes remained underground, unaffected by military actions that destroyed grain fields by trampling. The farmer who knew where the potatoes had been growing could dig them up as needed and feed his family. Soon people in Ireland were eating about 8 pounds of potatoes per person per day, and including potatoes in every meal. This new tradition allowed an increase in Ireland's population from less than a million to more than 8 million by 1845.

Then catastrophe struck. It was not military action, but a fungus disease. Called "the late blight," it invaded the leaves, killed the top of the plant, and progressed underground, destroying the tubers and the roots too. So complete was the failure of the Irish potato crop in 1845 and 1846 that more than a million Irish people died of starvation, or of diseases that became killers because of the famine. Emigration from Ireland to the United States alone jumped from about 4,000 annually to 61,242 in 1845, 105,953 in 1846, and doubled again in 1847. This emigration continued throughout the rest of the century, bringing the Irish population to about 4 million.

If we compare the principal starchy foods that people eat in various countries, examining the nutritional value of each (see table on page 185) as a dietitian would, we see that traditional choices show no relation to their content of carbohydrates, fats, needed components of proteins, minerals or vitamins. Particularly strange is the attitude toward millet in North America and Europe. Despite its excellence as a source of food, especially of the essential amino acids which the human body cannot synthesize as needed, we regard millet as bird

Per 100 grams (Approximately 4 ounces)

Columns are grouped as: Energy Available, Carbohydrates, Fats, Total Proteins | ESSENTIAL AMINO ACIDS —— WITH SPARING ACTION | MINERALS | VITAMINS (B VITAMINS)

Per 100 g	Energy Available (Cals)	Carbohydrates (g)	Fats (g)	Total Proteins (g)	Isoleucine (g)	Leucine (g)	Lysine (g)	Methionine (g)	Phenylalanine (g)	Threonine (g)	Tryptophane (g)	Valine (g)	Cystine (g)	Tyrosine (g)	Calcium (mg)	Iron (mg)	Vitamin A (IU)	Thiamine (mg)	Riboflavin (mg)	Niacin (mg)	Vitamin C (mg)
Barley, pearled	349	78.8	1.0	12.8	.54	.89	.42	.18	.66	.43	.16	.64	.26	.47	16	2.0	—	.12	.05	3.1	—
Corn flour, white	377	76.8	2.6	7.8	.36	1.01	.22	.14	.45	.31	.05	.51	.10	**.61**	6	1.8	tr.	.20	.06	1.4	—
Millet, pearl	327	72.9	2.9	11.4	.64	1.74	.38	**.29**	.51	.46	**.25**	.53	.15	—	20	**6.8**	—	**.73**	**.38**	2.3	—
Millet, proso	—	—	—	—	—	—	—	—	—	—	—	—	—	—	—	—	—	—	—	—	—
Oatmeal	**390**	68.2	**7.4**	**14.2**	**.73**	1.06	**.52**	.21	**.76**	**.47**	.18	**.84**	**.31**	.52	**53**	4.5	—	.60	.14	1.0	—
Potato, raw	76	17.1	0.1	2.0	.09	.10	.11	.02	.09	.08	.02	.11	.02	.04	7	.6	tr.	.10	.04	1.5	**20**
Potato, baked	93	21.1	0.1	2.6	—	—	—	—	—	—	—	—	—	—	9	.7	tr.	.10	.04	1.7	**20**
Rice, raw white	363	**80.4**	0.4	6.7	.36	.66	.30	.14	.38	.30	.08	.53	.10	.04	24	.8	—	.07	.03	1.6	—
Rice, cooked wh.	109	24.2	0.1	2.0	—	—	—	—	—	—	—	—	—	—	—	—	—	—	—	—	—
Rye flour, light	357	77.9	1.0	9.4	.40	.63	.38	.15	.44	.35	.10	.49	.19	.30	22	1.1	—	.15	.07	.6	—
Sorghum grain	332	73.0	3.3	11.0	.60	**1.77**	.30	.19	.55	.39	.12	.63	.18	.30	28	4.4	—	.38	.15	3.9	—
Wheat flour, whole	333	71.0	2.0	13.3	.58	.89	.36	.20	.62	.38	.16	.62	.29	.50	41	3.3	—	.55	.12	**4.3**	—

(shown by figures in boldface, the greatest content among these foods; shown by figures in italics, the least content)

Total protein and amino acid data from *Amino Acid Content of Foods* by M. L. Orr and B. K. Watt, U. S. Department of Agriculture, Home Economics Research Report No. 4, Dec. 1957. 82 pp.

Other data from *Composition of Foods: Raw, Processed, Prepared* by B. K. Watt and A. L. Merrill, U. S. Department of Agriculture, Agriculture Handbook No. 8, Dec. 1963 revision. 190 pp.

seed. In Africa and parts of Asia where millet is used in human diets, it is often considered a poor man's food, one not so desirable as less nutritious grains. It should be noted that rice, in particular, loses much of its value if the water in which it is cooked is not used.

The list might have been extended to include manioc (or cassava), a plant native to tropical America; and taro (or dasheen), which is native to the East Indies and is the source of the Hawaiian poi. Both of these plants grow in marshy or swampy places under primitive cultivation. Certain palms and palmlike cycads yield sago starch from their pithy centers. All of these foods are poor in nutritional values, particularly in the essential amino acids.* The protein-deficiency disease known as kwashiorkor is especially common among people whose principal starch is from taro, manioc, sago, rice and maize in tropical America, or maize in Africa.

Until people try living in foreign lands and eating the native foods for month after month, they rarely realize how deeply their personal preferences are rooted to the traditions of their childhood. A person whose idea of a good meal is one containing meat and potatoes is severely challenged to be satisfied for long on rice and beans, or corn meal products, or millet porridge. The bland, starchy, stomach-filling ingredients have much in common. Yet their differences become magnified as the weeks go by. Tolerance for the foreign dishes then tends to depend upon enjoyment of the less starchy and more flavorful components of each meal.

Often the botanist regards as a fruit a food that is called a vegetable. Tomatoes are "vegetables" when cooked (stewed or baked) but fruits when eaten raw. Generally the location in which the plant itself stores its sugars and starches determines which organ will be the potential food for man. The

---

* Cassava flour contains in each 100 grams only 1.6 of protein: 0.01 of methionine and of tryptophane, 0.02 of cystine, 0.03 of isoleucine, of threonine and of tyrosine, 0.04 of phenylalanine, 0.05 of valine, and 0.07 of leucine and of lysine.

geographical origin of major edible plants, or those used for flavoring or beverages, is shown in the table on pages 188–89.

The impact of tradition upon the foods we eat, the flavorings we enjoy, and the beverages we drink can be seen in the fact that so few new ones have been added as a consequence of world exploration. The discovery of Australia, for example, extended the acquaintance of botanists to thousands of plant species that had hitherto been unknown. But except for the Queensland nut (*Macadamia*) as an edible seed and eucalyptus oil as a powerful fragrance, none became popular elsewhere in the world for food or flavoring. From the New World too, the useful plants in these categories have had a mixed reception. Virtually all of them were under cultivation, however unscientific and casual, when explorers from Europe began visiting the Americas. Yet their adoption often followed strange paths. Tomatoes, for example, reached Europe as curiosities under the enticing name of "love apple." For a while they were forbidden fruit, which tempted many to taste them. Much more recently they were found to be not only delicious but an important source of Vitamin C.

The introduction of bananas from the Old World for cultivation in the tropics of the Americas held far greater hope for economic gains than any program to promote the sale of tropical fruits native to the New World. Nor have "white man's foods" that originated around the eastern Mediterranean found much appeal among peoples of the Far East. The ease with which these plants can be cultivated or the nutritional values available in their products cannot compete with traditions in diet.

Curiously, the substances of plant origin with the least value in nutrition are the ones for which man has been willing to go farthest. Hazardous voyages were undertaken to find the "Spice Islands" where black pepper originated. Colonial powers expanded their land holdings in the tropics to have places in which to cultivate coffee and tea, cacao and vanilla, and to have reliable sources of ginger, nutmeg and cloves.

Industrial organizations in the Western World have been

	NORTH AMERICAN SUBKINGDOM	NORTHERN EURASIAN SUBKINGDOM	NEOTROPICAL KINGDOM	AFRICAN SUBKINGDOM	SOUTHERN ASIAN SUBKINGDOM
Cereals		barley[7] millet[7] oats[7] rye[7] sorghum[7] wheat[7]	maize[7]	millet[7] sorghum[7] wheat[7]	rice[7]
Vegetables		asparagus[2] beet[1] broccoli[6] cabbage[4] carrot[1] celery[5] lettuce[4] onion[4] parsley[5] parsnip[1] pea[8] radish[1] spinach[5] turnip[1]	"Irish" potato[2] kidney bean[8] lima bean[8] manioc[1] peppers[7] pumpkin[7] squash[7] yam[1]	bread fruit[7] broad bean[8]	egg plant[7] soy bean[8] taro[1]
Fruits and Seeds	blackberry[7] blueberry[7] cherry[7] cranberry[7] pecan[8] persimmon[7] plum[7] strawberry[7]	almond[8] apple[7] cherry[7] currant[7] date[7] fig[7] gooseberry[7] grape[7] melon[7] mulberry[7] olive[7] pear[7] plum[7] quince[7] strawberry[7]	avocado[7] Brazil nut[8] cashew[8] chayote[7] coconut[8] grapefruit[7] guava[7] papaya[7] peanut[7] persimmon[7] pineapple[7] tomato[7]	gooseberry[7] grape[7] pistachio[8] watermelon[7]	apricot[7] banana[7] cantaloupe[7] citron[7] cucumber[7] date[7] lemon[7] lime[7] mango[7] orange[7] peach[7] plantain[7] plum[7]

	NORTH AMERICAN SUBKINGDOM	NORTHERN EURASIAN SUBKINGDOM	NEOTRO-PICAL KINGDOM	AFRICAN SUB-KINGDOM	SOUTHERN ASIAN SUB-KINGDOM
Flavorings and Bev- erages	sage[5] sassafras[2,3] winter- green[5]	caraway[8] celery seed[8] dill[2,4,5,8] garlic[4] hops[6] horse- radish[1] mustard[8] pepper- mint[5] spearmint[5]	cacao[8] (choc- olate) mate[2,4,5] tobacco[5]	coffee[8] cola[7]	almond[8] camphor[2] cinnamon[3] cloves[4] ginger[2] nutmeg[8] pepper[7] sesame[8] tea[5]

(Superscript numbers indicate the important part or parts of each plant: 1 = root, 2 = stem, 3 = bark, 4 = bud, 5 = leaf, 6 = flower cluster, 7 = fruit, and 8 = seed.)

willing to go farther and be much more experimental about plant products that could be used for purposes less limited by tradition. If the treatment of malaria could be improved by use of quinine extracted from the bark of the cinchona tree to be found scattered through the rain forests of tropical America, this material should be sought out. If a clear oil from the seeds of the chaulmoogra trees in the East Indies could help slow the course of degeneration in leprosy, it too should be obtained in the most efficient manner. If the milky latex that could be gathered from cuts in the bark of the Brazilian rubber tree would make good rubber, additional plantations of the best trees should be set out in West Africa, the East Indies, or anywhere else that they would grow well. Today the critical features in finding value in fibers from plants is the length and strength, the cost of producing them and the price that can be obtained.

The stems of hemp, jute and ramie from southern Europe and Asia Minor provide strong fibers of commercial importance,

Banana plant
and a rubber tree being tapped

competing strongly with sisal from century plants of tropical America and abacá from a member of the banana family in southern Asia. Useful fibers from flax plants were put to use long ago in both regions where it is native: across Eurasia and North Africa, where it was the source of materials for linen thread and the preferred "rags" for making rag paper of high quality; and in the southwestern United States. As an additional value, the seeds of the flax plant ("linseed" or linen seed) contain a valuable oil ("linseed oil") used in making paints.

Cotton seeds were being stripped of their long white hairs to be made into thread and then into cotton cloth by Hindus before 1800 B.C. Additional kinds of cotton were discovered in tropical and subtropical America, including kinds known as sea-island cotton, Jamaica cotton, and upland cotton. Since the invention of the cotton-gin in 1793, for separation of the fibers from the seeds, cotton has become the world's most widely used textile. Cotton seeds yield a valuable oil, and the residue (called oil-cake) is a nourishing food for livestock. For stuffing pillows and mattresses, the silky fibers from the seeds of the silk-cotton tree are often preferred. Known as kapok, it is a contribution from a sturdy plant native to the tropical rain forests in America. Kapok seeds yield an oil used in making soap.

The heaviest and most bulky crop that man harvests from the plant kingdom is wood. Its uses are almost endless: timbers for construction purposes on land or afloat; plywood where strength is wanted with a minimum of weight or bulk; veneers or solid pieces for furniture in which the grain, emphasized by appropriate stains, will add special beauty; pulpwood for paper-making; fence posts and railroad ties; and as a fuel that can be obtained and handled more easily than coal, petroleum or natural gas.

Actually, the use of wood in the Far East eliminated the supply and, in eastern China, forced people on the flood plains of the great rivers to manage with poorer fuels. This, in turn, brought them to a diet dominated by rice. In industrialized parts of the Western World, substitutes had to be found for timbers in construction of large buildings. By 1750 the supply of wood available as fuel to the iron industry had diminished to the point where an end to smelting operations seemed in sight. The first attempts at burning soft coal often ended in disaster, through production of carbon monoxide and other gases that asphyxiated the workers, or by sudden explosions of coal dust mixed with air. Not until around 1800 were ways found to get the energy from fossil fuels with reasonable safety. By then, men had grown used also to disasters in coal mines and were willing to take their chances digging coal to earn a living.

DANGEROUS PLANTS

Only in science fiction are stories told of carnivorous plants reaching out and seizing people. On a smaller scale and as fascinating exceptions to the ordinary behavior of plants, the Venus flytrap of the coastal Carolinas does close its leaf blades rather suddenly around ants and flies. The sundews of all continents do curl their tentacle-like leaf edges around insects and then digest them. The pitcher plants of several different types from the northern taiga country to the Australian bush do capture and get nourishment from small animals that tumble into the water held by the leaves. Bladderworts and similar vegetation in freshwater shallows catch mosquito wrigglers and other swimmers of small size. And a few fungi capture roundworms in the soil, snaring them in tight coils that constrict when the worm nudges against the plant. In each of these examples the plant is larger than its prey.

In relation to mankind, the dangerous plants are mostly

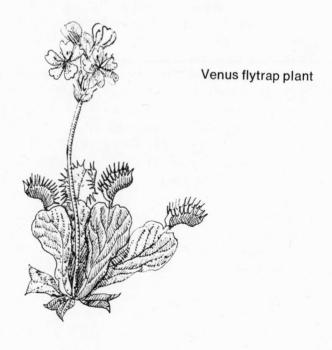

Venus flytrap plant

the small ones: bacteria that cause fatal diseases, fungi such as those that cause "athlete's foot" and "ringworm" of the scalp, or fleshy reproductive parts that might be edible but prove (as do some mushrooms and some fruits) to be deadly poisonous. Only in the last century has an acceptance of the "germ theory" of disease led to use in the advanced countries of methods in public health that reduce the chance of contagion, and in medical treatment of infected individuals to speed their recovery. In many countries, some of them as close as Latin America, so little has been accomplished, despite the availability of knowledge, that employed people lose an average of 15 percent of their working time each year to communicable diseases that are almost unknown in the United States, Canada, Great Britain, and many industrialized nations elsewhere.

DESTRUCTIVE PLANTS

To a small farmer anywhere in the world, who sees his family dying of starvation because some fungus disease has ruined the crop upon which his fortunes hang, the distinction between a dangerous plant and a destructive one is almost meaningless. The same is true for people in the Far East, who starve to death because moisture and fungi get to the grain donated by other countries for famine relief, and destroy it before it can be distributed and eaten. Where human death is the consequence, the word destructive (rather than dangerous) seems too mild.

Yet, for the most part, the destructive plants are merely the parasites and decomposers that serve important roles in nature. Under normal circumstances, the parasites help limit growth of populations before they exceed the space and nutrient resources that are available; parasites eliminate the susceptible and let the immune or unattacked plants reproduce the species. The decomposers hasten the day when the nutrient materials in plant cells that have no future can be returned to the earth. There the roots of growing plants can absorb them and use them in processes of lasting importance.

The entrance and activity of parasitic and decomposing plants used to be completely mysterious. But now that so much is known about both types, they can be regarded as pests that are to be excluded and controlled as much as possible for human benefit.

Often exclusion of pests must start at national or state boundaries, to prevent the introduction of a potential parasite before it starts to destroy anything. Failure to act in time allowed a fungus blight from the Orient to reach native chestnut trees in New York State in 1904. Oriental chestnuts are immune to it, but the American ones died until, within 35 years, scarcely a tree of this kind could be found in the eastern states. Meanwhile, in 1921, a disease of elms entered from the Netherlands and became known as the Dutch elm disease. It still causes American elms to die, row after row, when the fungus spreads through the interconnected root systems or is transported to healthy trees by bark beetles. So far, no way has been found to save these trees from the foreign fungi.

Native decomposers and parasites cause major destruction too. Foresters estimate that, by diminishing the rate of growth in infected trees and by rotting the heartwood, fungi actively reduce the supply of timber by about 45 percent. Some of these decomposers continue their activity in stored lumber and wooden buildings, making necessary expensive replacements whose dollar value is hard to estimate.

CONTROL OF PLANT PESTS

Plant pathologists, who examine carefully every stage in the life of the fungi that attack plants, seek always to discover practical ways in which the spread of a parasite or a decomposer can be blocked. Sometimes the parasite has developmental stages in two different hosts, of which one is a crop plant and the other a plant of lesser economic value. The blister rust of white pine, for example, goes through a stage on the foliage of currant or gooseberry bushes—members of the genus *Ribes*. By destroying all bushes of these kinds and forbidding their cultivation within a mile or more of white pine forests, the disease is kept to tolerable limits. Similarly the black rust of wheat has a developmental stage on barberry bushes, and causes much less damage if every bush of this kind is eradicated near wheat fields—within the distance that wind is likely to disperse the spores. Apple scab is just one manifestation of a fungus that first forms strange gall-like growths on juniper trees, such as the one called red cedar. Often this raises the problem of getting neighbors to agree on whether a county is going to profit most by raising scab-free apples or by producing red cedars for fence posts and railroad ties.

For a while, between 1950 and 1962, the chemical industries promoted a belief that with a suitable spray, any kind of plant pest could be controlled. To the man who owned the forest or made his living by raising a plant crop of shorter life span, "control" came close to his dream of exterminating the pest altogether. To reach this desirable situation, he was tempted to apply more of the dust or spray than would merely kill 95 percent of the infestation. Unfortunately, all of these programs had two effects that became increasingly evident. One was to bias the normal evolution of the pest until it became progressively more immune to the chemical added to the environment. The other was the contamination of plants, animals, soil and streams—even the ocean—with chemical compounds that affected many other forms of life adversely. Fungicides, insecticides, rodenticides, herbicides aimed at weeds that competed with the crop, all became known as biocides ("killers of life") and not just pesticides. Many of them decompose so slowly that their effects continue year after year, accumulating and polluting the world.

Techniques of breeding disease-resistant strains of the crop plant are slower and equally indecisive. The black rust of wheat, for example, appears in almost 150 different forms. Wheats can be bred that resist some but not all of these forms. As soon as a wheat is developed that seems immune to all forms of the wheat rust known from a particular region, new forms of the rust begin appearing and attacking with increased severity. Yet the wheat-raiser never feels that he should give up this endless battle. With the new wheat strains he can get 90 or 95 percent freedom from rust. With the old strains of wheat the damage rises to 50 percent or more as measured by lessened vigor in the wheat plants and a smaller yield of grain. The plant breeder, meanwhile, feels that he is being asked to act like a juggler, keeping many balls in the air at once without dropping one while picking up another. He is supposed to develop genetic strains of the crop plant that show increased resistance to the pest, without losing quality in the product, or diminishing the yield, or letting the plant become more susceptible to frost, drought, wind, animals or other hazards.

VANISHING PLANTS

Despite the fact that most trees outlive people, the plight of plants that are in danger of becoming extinct can be understood by considering these conspicuous members of the Plant Kingdom. In the Bible—I *Kings,* fifteenth chapter—we read about Solomon arranging with a neighboring monarch to let 80,000 hewers go from Israel to Lebanon, there to cut giant cedars and fashion timbers for the construction and ornamentation of the proposed palace and temple in Jerusalem. That occurred around 900 B.C. Today one small remnant of these famous forests is protected at Las Cedres, on the otherwise bald slopes of the Lebanon range. Without protection, the surviving trees would soon be felled for lumber and fuel. No new cedars would rise to take their place because hungry goats would eat every seedling before it grew tall and thick in the bark.

On the coast of California near Monterey are the last remnants of forests that grew there a century ago, dominated by the local Monterey pine (*Pinus radiata*). The surviving groves are protected from man, but not from the erosive forces of the Pacific Ocean, which continues to carve away the headlands on which the Monterey pines still grow. But at the same time, man is not permitting new forests of this endemic tree to rise

A Monterey pine deformed by coastal wind and spray

on suitable land farther from the water. There he favors other
trees of greater market value. Instead, the Monterey pine is
gaining a new lease on life as an introduced species suitable
for afforestation projects in South Africa and New Zealand—
on land where no pine of any kind ever grew before.

The Lebanese with their cedars and the Californians with
their native pines had many years in which to notice their
forests shrink until the trees themselves reached the vanishing point. The people of Bermuda encountered a similar loss in
just a short time. Until 1944, millions of Bermuda cedars
formed handsome groves, shielding the islanders from wind
and intense sun. The cedar was the chief valuable tree, yielding a reddish-brown, knot-studded, aromatic wood. So resistant were the fibers of cedar wood that thin cross-sections

of large trees were used as flagstones, and planks of cedar were worked into fine, polished coffins as well as a multitude of souvenir items.

Local inspectors of the Bermuda Department of Agriculture failed to notice some scale insects on nursery plants imported in 1944. Soon the island entomologists were called upon to identify the insects, for they were killing cedars on and around the estate where the imported shrubs were set out. Attempts to exterminate the pests failed and, by 1949, it was apparent that no control would be possible. Funds that had been allocated toward protecting the remaining live cedars were redirected, to improve the appearance of the island by removing the unsightly gray trunks of dead trees. Few of Bermuda's native cedars survive. The whole appearance of the islands has changed. Erosion by wind and rain now threaten much of the exposed soil.

People who enjoy visiting groves of tall trees and who recognize the value of plants with this growth style in protecting the soil and conserving fresh water have been foresighted in several parts of the world. The most affluent and influential may well be those who joined to form the Save-the-Redwoods League in California. They pressed for legislative action to set aside some favorite areas as state and national parks, and collected funds with which to purchase other groves before the trees were cut for lumber. Disputes continue as to the intelligent use of land and forest resources. Conservationists regard the redwoods as a heritage to be enjoyed by present and future generations of people. Industrialists seek immediate financial gain by exploiting trees that no man planted, for they were seedlings before the beginning of the Christian era and cannot be replaced in fewer centuries. Since no attempt is made to regulate the rate of cutting to match the rate of replacement by new growth of equal quality, the redwood industry in recent years has been fighting for an assumed right to continue cutting until all useful unprotected trees of this kind are gone.

PLANTS AND THE SURVIVAL OF ALL LIFE

When Christopher Columbus discovered the forests on the island of Hispaniola (Haiti plus the Dominican Republic), his astonishment was written into the pages of his journal:

. . . And filled with trees of a thousand kinds and tall, and they seem to touch the sky. And I am told that they never lose their foliage, as I can understand, for I saw them green and lovely as they are in Spain in May. . . .

Three hundred and six years later, in 1799, the great plant geographer Alexander von Humboldt arrived with his botanist friend Aimé Bonpland on the north coast of South America. "What magnificent vegetation!" he wrote to a friend. "We have been running around like a pair of fools; for the first three days we weren't able to concentrate on anything." To-day, more than 25,000 kinds of trees alone are known from Latin America. On the mountain ranges of Mexico live thirty-five out of the world's ninety different species of pine trees. Fully a fourth of all the forests in the world now grow in this Neotropical Kingdom. Yet for various reasons,* utilization of these renewable resources remains at a low rate, and destruction is commoner than efficient use.

An appreciation for the many roles served by plants is as great a challenge to human intelligence as any other aspect of planning for the future. Most of the green vegetation in the world contributes to the oxygen of the air we breathe. Almost all of the energy that can be utilized by living things is cap-

---

* Only about 3 percent are softwoods (conifers), and hence easy to cut and use for construction lumber and pulpwood. The hardwood trees are mostly so scattered through dense, mixed stands that logging and extraction of preferred kinds are extremely costly. Much of the interior of the forest cannot be reached by road because, although the timber resource occupies about 15 percent of the world's land area, it is served by only about 3 percent of the world's road mileage. Scientific forestry, emphasizing careful management toward maximum yield for the longest possible time, has yet to be developed in most of Latin America.

tured from sunlight through photosynthesis. All other sources
of energy have a predictable end, when the cost of using
them will exceed the benefits to be gained. Plants subdue the
elemental forces of wave, and wind, and pelt of rain or hail.
They conserve, as well as use, the fresh waters upon which
land life depends. The nongreen plants renew the supply of
inorganic nutrients and maintain the soil in a form that can
nourish directly or indirectly most of the plants and animals
we know.

Beyond these fundamental contributions by plants to the
welfare of all life on earth, we recognize some special benefits
to human culture. Fashioned into canoes and ships and early
aircraft, the products of plants carried people to new destina-
tions. They provided the raw materials for shelters, utensils,
medicines, and the paper on which written records could
be kept and shared.

Some of the plants, through human choice, entered unwittingly into partnerships with mankind. They provide the
ingredients for edible meals and useful textiles, growing with
special luxuriance under human care, freeing the people from
a need to spend every waking moment in hunting for food
and fibers. No longer can most of these plants survive without protection. No longer can mankind sustain a civilization
without the cultivated plants.

Beyond the useful aspects of plants, people increasingly
appreciate their esthetic values. To balance the artificial environment of cities and of crop plants grown in pure stands
through techniques of monoculture, natural areas hold special
attraction. There, so far as possible, the wild flowers should
bloom in their season, the trees and shrubs give shade and
shelter as well as food to wild animals of all native kinds, and
the grasses of the prairie or the special vegetation of the
desert remain uncut. Seas free of pollution should surge
against shorelines where seaweeds of many kinds maintain
their place. Lakes should nourish freshwater life, and the
streams be clear, letting sunlight reach plants in running
water.

To have these living resources continue into an indefinite future requires a deliberate restraint today. The new view of our planet is a turn away from old measures of success—from increasing numbers of mankind and quantity of possessions—toward quality in the human environment. Quality means sharing the world's resources among nonhuman and unused kinds of life as well as among peoples and their live companions.

Index

About the Authors

LORUS and MARGERY MILNE have traveled over 600,000 miles on expeditions to North and Central America, Surinam, Europe, Africa, Southeast Asia, eastern Australia, New Zealand, and the South Pacific. They have lectured and conducted seminars at nine universities in South Africa, were UNESCO consultants in New Zealand, and have given talks, illustrated with their own films, for the National Audubon Society. Since 1960 they have participated in the Biological Sciences Curriculum Study program sponsored by the American Institute for Biological Sciences and the National Science Foundation.

Dr. Milne was born in Toronto, Canada, and graduated from the University of Toronto with honors in biology. He earned his M.A. and Ph.D. degrees in biology at Harvard University. He is now Professor of Zoology at the University of New Hampshire, where Mrs. Milne also teaches and conducts research. She was born in New York City and was graduated from Hunter College. She earned her first M.A. in biology at Columbia University and her second, also in biology, at Radcliffe College, where she took her Ph.D. in the same field.